CHINESE COOKING

BHS

Contents

Introduction

As in any other style of cooking, Chinese food is a symbol of life and good health, forming a central part of family and social activity for many people. Through cooking, one demonstrates personal inventiveness and creativity, as well as one's cultural background, so cooking can always be seen as a pleasurable activity.

In Chinese cooking, the preparation is of great importance. Many dishes require very fine chopping and shredding of the various ingredients, and they are combined in a very orderly manner. Those ingredients which are not easily available in the Western world can be substituted by others in the recipes. It is not necessary to use only Chinese utensils as these dishes can easily be prepared using basic kitchen equipment.

The main cooking technique used to produce good Chinese food is stir-frying. A wok is ideal, but a deep, non-stick pan will serve the purpose just as well. Stir-frying requires good temperature control and this is easily learnt through practice. The wok or pan should be heated, then the temperature reduced before adding oil. If the utensil is too hot the oil will burn, giving a charred, oily taste to the food, which may burn, too! The heat should be progressively raised for the addition of other ingredients. The whole process may take between five and seven minutes. Remember, never overcook, as this will not only destroy the crispness of the food, but also its flavour and goodness.

Chinese food incorporates six basic flavours, just like Indian food. They are: sweet, sour, salty, spicy, pungent and hot. Their employment and respective proportions must be well balanced. Flavouring is always supplemented by ready-prepared sauces, the most essential of which is soya sauce. Others commonly used are oyster and plum sauces.

Finally, garnishing should not be neglected, as presentation is every bit as important as preparation. After all, what appeals to the eye also appeals to the mind and thence to heart and stomach. A slice of cleverly carved carrot, a thin sliver of tomato and carefully arranged parsley or coriander, can add that all-important dash of colour.

Cooking is always a pleasure, especially Chinese cooking. It is a challenge and a way to explore one's creative talents. In any case, who does not want their efforts to be rewarded by the pleasure of an exquisite meal?

Finally, let me wish you many hours of sheer enjoyment in the exciting world of Chinese cuisine and, above all, the enjoyment of these gratifying meals.

Soups, Sauces and Dips

Plum Sauce

PREPARATION TIME: 10 minutes plus soaking overnight

COOKING TIME: 20-25 minutes

225g (8oz) dried apricot
225g (8oz) golden plums, fresh or canned, pitted
50g (2oz) raisins or sultanas
2.5cm (1 inch) fresh root ginger, peeled and shredded
175-225g (6-8oz) sugar
60ml (4 tblsp) white vinegar
2-3 dried red chillis
5ml (1 tsp) salt

Soak apricots overnight in sufficient water to completely cover. Drain apricots and reserve liquid. Mix apricots, plums, sultanas, ginger and sugar and add 250ml (8 fl oz) reserved apricot liquid. Bring to boil and lower heat to a gentle simmer. Simmer for 10-15 minutes until it is thick. Add vinegar and coarsely ground chillis to the sauce. Add salt and mix well to blend fruits. Cook for 5-10 minutes until thick and sticky. Cool and bottle.

Chilli Oil Dip

PREPARATION TIME: 5-8 minutes

COOKING TIME: 5 minutes

60ml (4 tblsp) cooking oil
2 cloves of garlic, bruised
3-4 coarsely ground dried red chillis
30ml (2 tblsp) sesame oil

Heat the cooking oil and fry garlic till dark brown. Remove garlic and discard. Add chillis and fry for a few seconds. Add sesame oil and remove from heat. Stir well and cool.

Ginger Dip

PREPARATION TIME: 5 minutes

120ml (4 fl oz) white malt vinegar
2 spring onions, chopped
2.5cm (1 inch) fresh root ginger, peeled and thinly sliced

Mix all the ingredients together and leave for 10-15 minutes before using.

Sweet and Sour Sauce

PREPARATION TIME: 5 minutes

COOKING TIME: 3-5 minutes

5ml (1 tsp) fresh root ginger, minced
15ml (1 tblsp) shredded leeks
60ml (4 tblsp) red or white vinegar
60ml (4 tblsp) sugar
Pinch of salt
2.5ml (½ tsp) light soya sauce
400ml (13 fl oz) water
15ml (1 tblsp) arrowroot or cornflour

Mix all the ingredients together in a pan and bring to the boil gently, stirring constantly until it thickens. The sauce should be smooth and clear.

This page, picture left: Sweet and Sour Sauce (top), Soya Dip (centre right) and Chilli Oil Dip (bottom). Picture right: Hoi Sin Sauce (top), Chilli Sauce (centre left) and Ginger Dip (bottom).

Facing page: Green Chilli and Ginger Dip (top), Garlic Dip (centre left) and Plum Sauce (bottom right).

Hoi Sin Sauce

PREPARATION TIME: 5 minutes

COOKING TIME: 8 minutes

This can be bought ready-made; the home-made variety does not have quite the same flavour.

15ml (1 tblsp) dark soya bean paste
2 cloves garlic, minced or very finely chopped
15ml (1 tblsp) sugar
2.5ml (½ tsp) salt
5ml (1 tsp) flour
2.5ml (½ tsp) chilli powder
450ml (¾ pint) red or white vinegar

Mix all the above ingredients together in a pan and bring to the boil. Simmer gently for 5-6 minutes or until it thickens. Cool and bottle.

Chilli Sauce

PREPARATION TIME: 5 minutes

COOKING TIME: 5 minutes

25g (1oz) dried red chillis, coarsely ground
50g (2oz) dried apricots, chopped
250ml (8 fl oz) red or white vinegar
5ml (1 tsp) salt
5ml (1 tsp) sugar
5ml (1 tsp) arrowroot or cornflour

Mix all the above ingredients together in a pan and bring to the boil. Simmer gently for 5 minutes until the sauce thickens. Cool and serve. Will keep bottled for a few weeks.

Garlic Dip

PREPARATION TIME: 5 minutes

45ml (3 tblsp) white vinegar
15ml (1 tblsp) minced garlic
Pinch sugar

Mix all the ingredients together and leave for 2 hours before using.

Soya Dip

PREPARATION TIME: 5 minutes

60ml (4 tblsp) light soya sauce
15ml (1 tblsp) dark soya sauce
2.5ml (½ tsp) sugar
2-3 green chillis, chopped
2-3 slices fresh root ginger, minced

Mix the above ingredients together and allow to stand for 10-15 minutes before using. Keep in an airtight glass jar.

Green Chilli and Ginger Dip

PREPARATION TIME: 5 minutes

4-5 green chillis, chopped
2.5cm (1 inch) fresh root ginger, peeled and finely sliced
2.5ml (½ tsp) salt
2.5ml (½ tsp) sugar
90ml (6 tblsp) malt vinegar

Mix above ingredients together and allow to stand for 2-3 hours before use.

Duck Soup

PREPARATION TIME: 10 minutes

COOKING TIME: 8 minutes

2 spring onions, finely chopped
15ml (1 tblsp) cooked oil, or standard cooking oil
2.5cm (1 inch) fresh root ginger, peeled and finely chopped
100g (4oz) cooked duck meat, chopped
100g (4oz) winter melon, thinly sliced
1½ litres (2½ pints) chicken stock
Salt to taste
Pinch monosodium glutamate (optional)
15ml (1 tblsp) Shao Hsing wine or dry sherry (optional)
5ml (1 tsp) arrowroot or cornflour blended with 15ml (1 tblsp) stock
Freshly ground black pepper to taste

Fry spring onions in the oil for 1 minute. Add ginger and duck meat. Stir-fry for 1 minute. Add winter melon and stir-fry for a further 1-2 minutes and then add stock and the remaining ingredients. Gently simmer for 2-3 minutes until the soup becomes clear. Serve immediately.

Wonton Soup

PREPARATION TIME: 10 minutes

COOKING TIME: 8 minutes

20-24 wontons
2 sprigs Chinese parsley, or watercress, finely chopped
1½ litres (2½ pints) chicken stock
2-3 spring onions, finely chopped
2.5cm (1 inch) fresh root ginger, peeled and finely chopped
Salt to taste
15ml (1 tblsp) soya sauce
Pinch monosodium glutamate (optional)
2.5ml (½ tsp) sugar
Few drops sesame oil
1.25ml (¼ tsp) ground white pepper

Boil wontons in a large saucepan of water for 2-3 minutes until they float to the surface. Remove and drain. Divide cooked wontons and parsley among 6-8 soup bowls. Bring stock to boil and add onions, ginger, salt and the remaining ingredients. Cook for 2-3 minutes, pour over the wontons and serve immediately.

Chicken and Mushroom Soup

PREPARATION TIME: 20 minutes

COOKING TIME: 6-8 minutes

100g (4oz) button mushrooms, sliced
50g (2oz) dried brown mushrooms, soaked and then sliced
50g (2oz) dried black mushrooms, soaked and then sliced
15ml (1 tblsp) oil
1½ litres (2½ pints) chicken stock
100g (4oz) shredded cooked chicken
3 spring onions, finely chopped
1.25ml (¼ tsp) monosodium glutamate (optional)
Salt to taste
15ml (1 tblsp) light soya sauce
10ml (2 tsp) Shao Hsing wine (optional)
Pinch ground white pepper
5ml (1 tsp) cornflour or arrowroot blended with 15ml (1 tblsp) stock

Stir fry the mushrooms in the oil for 2 minutes and then remove them. Bring the stock to the boil in a large pan with the remaining ingredients, apart from the cornflour and mushrooms, and simmer for 3-4 minutes. Add the blended cornflour and the mushrooms, and simmer for 1-2 minutes. Serve immediately.

Egg Drop Soup

PREPARATION TIME: 10 minutes

COOKING TIME: 8 minutes

This soup derives its name from stirring beaten eggs into the boiling hot soup. On hitting the soup, the egg cooks and forms threads. The eggs can also be carefully dropped in whole, so that they cook without breaking in the hot soup.

1½ litres (2½ pints) chicken stock
3 spring onions, finely chopped
75g (3oz) frozen peas, or shelled fresh peas
1 bunch watercress, finely chopped
A few thin slices of fresh root ginger
Salt and freshly ground black pepper to taste
15ml (1 tblsp) light soya sauce
Pinch of monosodium glutamate (optional)
5ml (1 tsp) cornflour blended with 15ml (1 tblsp) water
4 eggs, beaten (or 6-8 whole eggs, see below)

Bring the chicken stock to the boil with the spring onions, peas, watercress, ginger and salt and pepper to taste. Allow to simmer for 2-3 minutes. Add the soya sauce, monosodium glutamate and the blended cornflour. Stir well until the soup is transparent and thick. Bring the soup back to the boil and stir in the beaten eggs. Serve immediately. Alternatively, put a whole egg into each warm soup bowl and ladle the hot soup over the top.

Duck Soup (top), Chicken and Mushroom Soup (centre right) and Wonton Soup (right).

Chicken Noodle Soup

PREPARATION TIME: 10 minutes

COOKING TIME: 10-12 minutes

450g (1lb) Shanghai noodles, or very
    thin noodles
30ml (2 tblsp) oil
225g (8oz) cooked chicken, cubed
175g (6oz) Chinese white cabbage or
    ordinary white cabbage, shredded
1½ litres (2½ pints) chicken stock

Seasoning
2.5ml (½ tsp) sugar
2.5ml (½ tsp) salt
10ml (2 tsp) Shao Hsing wine
    (optional)
2.5ml (½ tsp) monosodium
    glutamate
10ml (2 tsp) light soya sauce

Add the noodles to a large pan of
boiling water. Stir to loosen the
bundles and boil for 4-5 minutes.
(The noodles should be just tender
but not overcooked.) Drain
noodles well. Meanwhile, heat the
oil in the wok and fry the chicken
for 1-2 minutes. Remove the
chicken and then fry the cabbage in
the same oil for 2 minutes. Add the
seasoning ingredients and stir fry
for 1 minute. Add the chicken and
cook for a further 1-2 minutes until
the cabbage is tender. Add the
stock and bring to the boil. Divide
noodles among 6-8 warm soup
bowls and add the hot soup. Serve
immediately.

Chinese Parsley and Fish Soup

PREPARATION TIME: 10 minutes

COOKING TIME: 7-8 minutes

450g (1lb) white fish fillet, cut into 6
    even-sized pieces
1 litre (1¾ pints) chicken stock
1cm (½ inch) fresh root ginger, peeled
    and thinly sliced
Salt to taste
Freshly ground black pepper to taste
Pinch monosodium glutamate
    (optional)
2 spring onions, finely chopped
2.5ml (½ tsp) arrowroot or cornflour
2 sprigs Chinese parsley, finely
    chopped
18-20 thin cucumber slices

Wash fish in cold water and gently
simmer in chicken stock for 2-3
minutes. Remove the fish pieces
carefully. Add ginger, salt, pepper,
MSG and onion and simmer the

stock for 2-3 minutes. Strain.
Dissolve arrowroot in 15ml (1
tblsp) of water or cold stock and
add to the soup. Simmer for 2
minutes until the soup thickens.
Add fish pieces and bring back to
the boil. Serve in soup bowls,
sprinkled with chopped parsley
and cucumber slices.

Crab and Watercress Soup

PREPARATION TIME: 10 minutes

COOKING TIME: 8-9 minutes

1½ litres (2½ pints) chicken stock
100g (4oz) white crab meat,
    shredded
2 spring onions, finely chopped
2 bunches watercress, finely chopped
Salt and freshly ground black pepper
    to taste
5ml (1 tsp) cornflour or arrowroot
15ml (1 tblsp) water
10ml (2 tsp) light soya sauce
A few drops sesame oil

Bring the stock to the boil with the
crab meat, onions and watercress
and simmer for 4-5 minutes. Add

salt and pepper to taste. Mix the
cornflour with the water and add
to the soup. Allow to simmer for a
further 2 minutes. Add soya sauce
and sesame oil, mix well and
simmer for 2 minutes. Serve
immediately.

Crab and Sweet Corn Soup

PREPARATION TIME: 8 minutes

COOKING TIME: 8 minutes

45ml (3 tblsp) water or stock
30ml (2 tblsp) cornflour or arrowroot
1½ litres (2½ pints) chicken stock
275-350g (10-12oz) creamed sweet
    corn
100-175g (4-6oz) crab meat,
    shredded
Salt and freshly ground black pepper
    to taste
5ml (1 tsp) soya sauce
Pinch monosodium glutamate
    (optional)

Blend water and cornflour
together. Bring the stock to the boil
in a large pan. Add the sweet corn,
crab, salt and pepper to taste, soya

sauce and monosodium glutamate.
Simmer for 4-5 minutes. Add the
blended cornflour to the soup and
stir over a gentle heat until the
soup thickens. Serve immediately.
Whisked egg whites can be stirred
into the hot soup just before
serving, if liked.

Hot and Sour Soup

PREPARATION TIME: 20 minutes

COOKING TIME: 7-8 minutes

1½ litres (2½ pints) chicken stock
50g (2oz) pork, shredded, or cubed
    barbecued pork
50g (2oz) peeled shrimps
25g (1oz) bamboo shoots, sliced
2 cloud ear fungus, soaked in boiling
    water for 5 minutes and chopped
2-3 spring onions, chopped
Salt to taste
15ml (1 tblsp) sugar
2.5ml (½ tsp) monosodium glutmate
    (optional)
5ml (1 tsp) dark soya sauce
2.5ml (½ tsp) light soya sauce
22.5ml (1½ tblsp) malt vinegar
5ml (1 tsp) chilli oil or chilli sauce
1.25ml (¼ tsp) sesame oil
2.5ml (½ tsp) Shao Hsing wine
    (optional)
1 egg, well beaten
15ml (1 tblsp) cornflour or arrowroot
30ml (2 tblsp) water

Mix stock with pork, shrimps, and
all the remaining ingredients except
the well-beaten egg, cornflour and
water. Simmer gently for 4-5
minutes. Remove from heat and
add the egg, stirring gently, until
the egg forms 'threads' in the soup.
Blend the cornflour with the water
and add to the soup. Simmer for 1
minute until the soup thickens and
serve immediately.

**This page: Egg Drop Soup (top),
Crab and Watercress Soup
(centre) and Crab and Sweet
Corn Soup (bottom).**

**Facing page: Chicken Noodle
Soup (top), Hot and Sour Soup
(centre left) and Chinese Parsley
and Fish Soup (bottom right).**

Snacks

Four Happiness Dumplings

PREPARATION TIME: 30-45 minutes for pastry; 20-30 minutes for filling

COOKING TIME: 20 minutes

Pastry
225g (8oz) plain flour
Pinch of salt
200ml (⅓ pint) boiling water

Put the flour and salt into a bowl. Add the boiling water and mix quickly to make a dough. Cover and allow to stand for 20-30 minutes. Knead the dough for 2-3 minutes, sprinkling the work surface with a little cornflour if needed. Divide the dough into 30-35 equal portions and roll each one to a circle 6cm (2½") in diameter.

Filling
175g (6oz) boned loin of pork, finely chopped or minced
2 black mushrooms, soaked and diced
50g (2oz) mixed vegetables, peeled and finely chopped (peas, carrots, celery, etc.)
2.5ml (½ tsp) brown sugar or maltose
10ml (2 tsp) light soya sauce
1.25ml (¼ tsp) freshly ground black pepper
1 egg
5-6 chives, finely chopped
Salt to taste
15ml (1 tblsp) oil
7.5ml (1½ tsp) cornflour
30ml (2 tblsp) flour mixed with a little cold water to a smooth paste

Mix the pork with the mushrooms, mixed vegetables, sugar, soya sauce, black pepper, egg, chives and salt to taste. Add the oil and cornflour and mix well with a fork. Divide filling into 30 to 35 equal portions. Fill each dumpling wrapper with a portion of filling and shape into crescent shape dumplings. Steam them in an ordinary steamer or a Chinese bamboo steamer for about 20 minutes. Serve with a dip and chilli sauce. To make the crescent shape, place a wrapper on a flat surface, put a little filling in the centre, spread the edges with a little flour and water paste and pinch the edges of the wrapper together to seal. Pull one corner of the filled wonton around and over the other corner. Press to seal.

Steamed Shrimp Pancakes

PREPARATION TIME: 1 hour
COOKING TIME: 10-15 minutes

175g (6oz) plain flour or high gluten flour
50g (2oz) cornflour
1.25ml (¼ tsp) salt
15ml (1 tblsp) oil
45ml (3 tblsp) beaten egg
30ml (2 tblsp) water
30ml (2 tblsp) flour mixed with cold water to a smooth paste

Filling
150g (6oz) shrimps, boiled and finely chopped
2 spring onions, bulb only, finely chopped
1.25ml (¼ tsp) salt or to taste
5ml (1 tsp) cornflour to bind

Sieve the flour, cornflour and salt into a bowl. Add the oil, beaten egg and water and mix to make a stiff dough. Leave for 30 minutes to rest. Knead well for 5-6 minutes and roll into 25-30 15cm (6") circles on greaseproof paper. Place the filling in the centre and flatten. Spread flour and water paste around the edge of each pancake and fold up from one end to make a roll. Arrange the pancakes in a greased ordinary or Chinese bamboo steamer and cook over boiling water for 10-15 minutes. Serve piping hot with chilli or soya sauce dip.

Filling
To make the filling mix all the ingredients except the cornflour together, and then bind with the cornflour.

Alternative
To make rice pancakes, soak 100g (4oz) rice for 10 minutes. Grind with water to make a very fine paste of batter consistency. Add 15ml (1 tblsp) oil and mix well. Line a steamer with fine muslin and spoon in a little batter; spread it out into a thin pancake. Steam for 5 minutes. Place a little filling on the pancake and roll up. Steam for 10 minutes and serve piping hot with a dip.

Steamed Open Dumplings

PREPARATION TIME: 1 hour
COOKING TIME: 10-15 minutes

Filling
100g (4oz) peeled prawns, finely chopped
175g (6oz) pork or beef, minced
2 black mushrooms, soaked and finely chopped
Salt to taste
2.5ml (½ tsp) brown sugar

Seasoning
2.5ml (½ tsp) monosodium glutamate (optional)
15ml (1 tblsp) cornflour
5ml (1 tsp) dark soya sauce
5ml (1 tsp) light soya sauce
1.25ml (¼ tsp) freshly ground black pepper
15ml (1 tblsp) sesame oil
24 wonton wrappers

Mix the minced pork, prawns, mushrooms, salt and sugar together. Add the seasoning ingredients and mix well. Allow to stand for 30 minutes. Take each wonton wrapper and spoon a little filling in the centre. Fold up the edges around the filling but do not completely enclose it. (An open ended dumpling is produced with the sides of the wrapper gathered around the filling.) Flatten the base by pressing it slightly so that it will stand upright in a steamer. Grease an ordinary steamer or a bamboo steamer and arrange the dumplings in it. Steam for 15-20 minutes. Serve hot with a dip.

Wontons with Pork and Shrimp Filling

PREPARATION TIME: 30 minutes

COOKING TIME: 10-15 minutes

175g (6oz) lean pork, minced
Oil
175g (6oz) peeled shrimps, finely chopped
3 spring onions, finely chopped
2.5ml (½ tsp) ground white pepper
15ml (1 tblsp) soya sauce
7.5ml (1½ tsp) rice wine or dry sherry
2.5ml (½ tsp) salt, or to taste
7.5ml (1½ tsp) cornflour blended with 30ml (2 tblsp) water
40-50 wonton wrappers
30ml (2 tblsp) plain flour, mixed with a little cold water to a smooth paste

Fry pork in 30ml (2 tblsp) oil until it loses its pink colour. Add shrimps and onions and fry for 3-4 minutes. Add pepper, soya sauce and wine. Season with salt and stir fry for 1-2 minutes. Add the blended cornflour and stir over a moderate heat until thickened. Allow to cool before filling the wontons. Divide filling into 40-50 equal portions. Take a wonton wrapper, moisten the edges with the flour and water paste. Place a portion of filling in the centre of the wonton and gather up the edges to make a neat round, or shape in such a way as to make a triangle or any other shape that you prefer. Once you have shaped all the wontons, deep-fry them in hot oil until crisp and golden. You will need to fry them in 3 or more batches. Drain well on absorbent paper before serving.

Fried Meat Dumplings

PREPARATION TIME: 10 minutes
COOKING TIME: about 15 minutes

30ml (2 tblsp) cooking oil
225g (8oz) lean, minced beef or lamb
2 spring onions, chopped
30ml (2 tblsp) light soya sauce
2.5ml (½ tsp) salt
22.5ml (1½ tblsp) rice wine or dry sherry
10ml (2 tsp) cornflour mixed with 30ml (2 tblsp) water

Dumpling wrappers (see recipe)
30ml (2 tblsp) plain flour mixed to a paste with cold water
Oil for deep frying

Heat the 30ml (2 tblsp) oil in a pan and fry the minced meat and onion for 2-3 minutes. Add the soya sauce, salt and wine. Cook gently for 2 minutes and then stir in the cornflour and water mixture. Stir over the heat until the mixture thickens. Put the meat mixture into a dish and leave to cool. Divide into equal portions – about 48. Take a round dumpling wrapper and place a portion of filling in the centre. Moisten the edges of the wrapper with a little flour and water paste, gather the edges up and over the filling and pinch together to seal. Shape neatly. Continue to make the remaining

dumplings in the same way. Deep-fry the dumplings in moderately hot oil, cooking a few dumplings at a time, until they are golden brown. Drain thoroughly on absorbent paper. Serve with chilli sauce dip.

Dumpling Wrappers
(Chiao Tze P'i)
PREPARATION TIME: 50-60 minutes

275g (10oz) plain flour
200ml (⅓ pint) cold water

Makes 40-50 wrappers

Sieve the flour into a bowl and add the cold water, a little at a time, and mix to a firm dough. Knead the dough on a flat surface for 4-5

minutes. Cover with a damp cloth or wrap in cling film. Leave to stand at room temperature for 30-40 minutes. Roll out on a well-floured surface as thinly as possible, until almost transparent. Cut into round or square pieces to suit your requirements. Use within a few hours of making otherwise they will dry out.

Wonton Wrappers

PREPARATION TIME: 5-6 hours (including standing time)

120g (4¼oz) high gluten flour
30ml (2 tblsp) beaten egg
30ml (2 tblsp) cold water
Cornflour
Makes 40-50 wrappers

Sieve flour and gradually add the beaten egg and water mixed together. Mix to a stiff dough. Knead firmly for 5-6 minutes and wrap in cling film. Leave to stand at room temperature for 4-5 hours. Roll out into a very large square on a work surface dusted with cornflour. The pastry should be almost transparent. Cut into 40-50 7.5cm (3″) round or square wrappers. Dust each wrapper with cornflour before stacking. Store the wrappers, wrapped securely in cling film, in the refrigerator, for up to 24 hours. If they are allowed to dry out they will split during cooking.

Spring Roll Wrappers

PREPARATION TIME: 20 minutes, plus chilling time

100g (4oz) strong plain flour
1 egg, beaten
A little cold water

Makes 12 wrappers

Sieve the flour into a bowl. Make a well in the centre and add the beaten egg and a little cold water. Mix to a soft yet firm dough, adding a little extra water if necessary. Knead the dough until it is really pliable. (This helps to make the gluten work.) Chill, covered, for 4 hours or overnight. Allow to come back to room temperature. Roll out the dough on a well-floured surface to about 5mm (¼″) thick. Cut into 12 equal pieces, and then roll each piece to a square about 15x15cm (6x6″) – each square should be very thin.

Spring Rolls

PREPARATION TIME: 20-30 minutes

COOKING TIME: about 20 minutes

225g (8oz) lean, raw pork or beef, finely shredded
100g (4oz) prawns or shrimps (either uncooked or boiled), shelled
4 spring onions, finely chopped
Cooking oil
10ml (2 tsp) fresh root ginger, peeled and shredded
100g (4oz) white cabbage, shredded
75g (3oz) bean sprouts
15ml (1 tblsp) soya sauce
Salt to taste
12 spring roll wrappers, each 15cm (6″) square (see recipe)
30ml (2 tblsp) plain flour, mixed with a little cold water to a smooth paste

Fry the shredded pork, prawns or shrimps and the spring onions in 15ml (1 tblsp) of cooking oil for 2-3 minutes. Add the ginger, cabbage and bean sprouts, and stir fry for 2-3 minutes. Add soya sauce, and season with a little salt if desired. Remove from the heat and allow to cool. Lay out the spring roll wrappers on a clean working surface, with one point of each wrapper facing you. Divide the

filling mixture into 12 equal portions and place one portion of filling just above the front point of each wrapper. Fold in the opposite side points, so that they overlap slightly like an envelope – secure the side points with a little flour and water paste. Starting with the point facing you, roll each wrapper up around the filling, securing the remaining point with a little flour

and water paste. Repeat in exactly the same way with the remaining spring roll wrappers. They will keep a better shape if you chill them for 1 hour before cooking. Deep fry over a medium heat until golden brown and crisp. Drain thoroughly on absorbent paper and serve hot with a selection of dips or chilli sauce. The spring rolls can be frozen, uncooked.

This page: Fried Meat Dumplings (top right), Spring Rolls (centre left) and Wontons with Pork and Shrimp Filling (bottom). Facing page: Spiced Beef (top), Steamed Beef Szechuan Style (bottom left) and Beef with Green Pepper and Chilli (bottom right).

Meat Dishes

Spiced Beef

PREPARATION TIME: 30 minutes

COOKING TIME: 5-6 minutes

Marinade
5ml (1 tsp) sugar
2-3 star anise, ground
2.5ml (½ tsp) ground fennel
15ml (1 tblsp) dark soya sauce
*1.25ml (¼ tsp) monosodium
  glutamate (optional)*

*450g (1lb) fillet of beef, cut into
  2.5cm (1″) strips*
*2.5cm (1″) fresh root ginger, peeled
  and crushed*
2.5ml (½ tsp) salt
30ml (2 tblsp) oil
4 spring onions, sliced
*2.5ml (½ tsp) freshly ground black
  pepper*
15ml (1 tblsp) light soya sauce

Mix the marinade ingredients
together. Add the beef strips,
ginger and salt, and marinate for 20
minutes. Heat the oil in wok and
stir fry the onions for 1 minute.
Add beef, ground pepper and soya
sauce and stir fry for 4-5 minutes.
Serve with a dip.

Steamed Beef Szechuan Style

PREPARATION TIME: 40 minutes

COOKING TIME: 15 minutes

3 slices fresh root ginger, minced
5ml (1 tsp) salt
5ml (1 tsp) sugar
Freshly ground black pepper
15ml (1 tblsp) oil
30ml (2 tblsp) rice wine or dry sherry
22.5ml (1½ tblsp) chilli bean paste
30ml (2 tblsp) dark soya sauce
3-4 spring onions, finely chopped
*450g (1lb) fillet of beef, cut into 5cm
  (2″) long strips*
100g (4oz) ground rice
*1 large lotus leaf or several cabbage
  leaves*

For the marinade, mix the ginger,
salt, sugar, pepper, oil, wine, bean
paste, soya sauce and half of the
spring onions. Add beef strips and
mix well. Leave to marinate for 15-

20 minutes. Heat the wok and dry-
roast the ground rice for 2-4
minutes till rice changes colour
from white to light brown. Roll the
marinated beef in the roasted
ground rice to give a thin, even
coating. Line the bamboo steamer
with a well-oiled lotus leaf or a few
old and tough cabbage leaves.
Arrange the coated beef strips in a
neat pile on top. Steam fairly

quickly for 10-15 minutes over
boiling water. Garnish with the
remaining chopped spring onions
before serving. Serve hot with chilli
sauce.

Beef with Green Pepper and Chilli

PREPARATION TIME: 30 minutes

COOKING TIME: 10-12 minutes

*450g (1lb) fillet of beef, cut into
  2.5cm (1″) strips*

Seasoning
30ml (2 tblsp) dark soya sauce
5ml (1 tsp) sesame oil
Pinch bicarbonate of soda
1.25ml (¼ tsp) ground black pepper
2.5ml (½ tsp) salt

Oil for cooking
2 green peppers, seeded and thinly sliced
1 onion, peeled and sliced
2 spring onions, chopped
2.5cm (1") fresh root ginger, peeled and sliced
2 garlic cloves, peeled and chopped
3 green chillis, sliced

Sauce
30ml (2 tblsp) chicken stock
2.5ml (½ tsp) monosodium glutamate (optional)
5ml (1 tsp) dark soya sauce
Salt to taste
Few drops sesame oil

Marinate beef with the seasoning ingredients for 15 minutes. Heat 30ml (2 tblsp) oil and stir fry green peppers and onions for 2 minutes. Remove to a plate. Reheat wok, add 30-45ml (2-3 tblsp) oil and fry ginger, garlic and green chillis for 1 minute. Add beef and stir fry for 4-5 minutes. Add sauce ingredients, mixed together, and the fried peppers and onions. Stir fry for a further 2 minutes and serve.

Diced Pork with Sweet Corn

PREPARATION TIME: 25 minutes
COOKING TIME: 15-20 minutes

Marinade
Pinch salt
10ml (2 tsp) dark soya sauce
1.25ml (¼ tsp) sugar
5ml (1 tsp) rice wine
15ml (1 tblsp) water

175g (6oz) pork loin, diced
Oil for deep frying
2 slices fresh root ginger, peeled and diced
1 clove garlic, peeled and chopped
250ml (8 fl oz) chicken stock

Seasoning
1.25ml (¼ tsp) salt
1.25ml (¼ tsp) freshly ground black pepper
1.25ml (¼ tsp) sugar
5ml (1 tsp) rice wine or dry sherry
Few drops sesame oil

5ml (1 tsp) cornflour mixed with 15ml (1 tblsp) water

250ml (8 fl oz) creamed *sweet corn*
1 egg, well beaten
4 spring onions, chopped

Mix the marinade ingredients together. Add the pork and leave to marinate for 15 minutes. Drain the pork and discard the liquid. Heat the wok and pour in the oil for deep frying. Fry the pork until light brown. Remove the pork and drain. Reserve the oil for future use. Heat 15ml (1 tblsp) oil in the wok, add the ginger and pork. Stir fry for 3 minutes. Add the stock and simmer for 3 minutes. Add the seasoning ingredients and simmer for 2-3 minutes. Add the blended cornflour and water and simmer until the sauce thickens. Add the sweet corn and beaten egg and cook for 2-3 minutes. Serve sprinkled with chopped onions. Serve this dish with plain boiled rice or noodles.

Pork Stuffed Mushrooms

PREPARATION TIME: 15-20 minutes
COOKING TIME: 12 minutes

Filling
1 egg
10ml (2 tsp) cornflour
10ml (2 tsp) rice wine or dry sherry
1.25ml (¼ tsp) minced fresh root ginger
6 water chestnuts, finely chopped
50g (2oz) peeled shrimps, chopped
175g (6oz) lean pork, minced
1.25ml (¼ tsp) salt
1.25ml (¼ tsp) freshly ground black pepper
2.5ml (½ tsp) sugar
10ml (2 tsp) chilli sauce

16 large, open mushrooms
600ml (1 pint) chicken stock
Oil

Mix all the filling ingredients together. Remove the mushroom stalks. Divide the filling into 16 portions. Bring the chicken stock to the boil. Add the mushrooms and leave to stand off the heat for 5 minutes, covered. Drain the mushrooms and discard the stock. Top each mushroom with a portion of filling. Put the stuffed mushrooms into a well-oiled steamer. Steam for 10-12 minutes over boiling water. Serve as a snack, as a starter or as a side dish. Alternatively, serve with a simple sauce made from thickened chicken broth. Pour the sauce over the steamed mushrooms.

Sliced Pork in Wine Sauce

PREPARATION TIME: 30 minutes

COOKING TIME: about 16 minutes

Seasoning
15ml (1 tblsp) red vinegar
15ml (1 tblsp) light soya sauce
15ml (1 tblsp) rice wine or dry sherry
10ml (2 tsp) soya paste
5ml (1 tsp) freshly ground black pepper
5ml (1 tsp) salt
5ml (1 tsp) Shao Hsing wine

450g (1lb) pork fillet, cut into 5cm (2″) long thin slices
15ml (1 tblsp) cornflour
60ml (4 tblsp) oil

2.5cm (½″) fresh root ginger, finely chopped
3 spring onions (or scallions), chopped
1 green pepper, seeded and diced

Sauce
10ml (2 tsp) cornflour
60ml (4 tblsp) dry white wine
120ml (4 fl oz) chicken stock
10ml (2 tsp) dark soya sauce
5ml (1 tsp) sugar
2.5ml (½ tsp) salt

Mix the seasoning ingredients together. Add the pork slices and leave to marinate for 10-15 minutes. Drain the pork and roll in the cornflour. Leave on one side. Discard the marinade. Heat half the oil in the wok until smoking. Add the pork, reduce the heat, and

Diced Pork with Sweet Corn (far left), Sliced Pork in Wine Sauce (top left) and Pork Stuffed Mushrooms (left).

**Steamed Pork with Salted Cabbage (top), Pork with
Green Pepper (centre right) and Pork Chop Suey (bottom).**

golden brown and tender. Remove
and drain on kitchen paper. Fry all
the meat balls and serve with
chopped spring onions and green
pepper rings sprinkled on top.
Serve as a snack, as a starter or as a
side dish.

Pork Chop Suey

PREPARATION TIME: 35 minutes

COOKING TIME: 10 minutes

Marinade
15ml (1 tblsp) water
2.5ml (½ tsp) bicarbonate of soda
10ml (2 tsp) dark soya sauce

*225g (½ lb) pork fillet, sliced into
   5cm (2″) pieces*
*45ml (3 tblsp) cooked oil or cooking
   oil*
1 onion, peeled and cut into pieces
1 clove of garlic, peeled and sliced
25g (1oz) bamboo shoots, sliced
175g (6oz) bean sprouts

Seasoning
Pinch salt
Pinch freshly ground black pepper
*Pinch monosodium glutamate
   (optional)*
45ml (3 tblsp) light soya sauce
5ml (1 tsp) sugar
5ml (1 tsp) cornflour

Sauce
5ml (1 tsp) cornflour
15ml (1 tblsp) water

Mix the marinade ingredients
together. Add the pork and leave
for 15 minutes to marinate. Drain
the pork and discard the marinade.
Heat the oil in the wok and stir fry
pork for 2-3 minutes. Remove the
pork. Add the onions, garlic and
bamboo shoots to the wok and stir
fry for 1-2 minutes. Add the
bean sprouts and stir fry for 2
minutes. Remove onto a dish and
add the mixed seasoning
ingredients. Leave for 10 minutes.
Return the pork and the vegetables
to the wok. Add the blended sauce
ingredients. Bring to the boil gently,
stirring until the sauce thickens.
Serve immediately.

stir fry for 4-6 minutes until lightly
browned. Remove the pork and
keep on one side. Discard any oil
left in the wok. Add the remaining
oil to the wok and stir fry the
onions, ginger and green pepper for
3-5 minutes. Return the fried pork
to the wok and cook for a further
2-3 minutes with the vegetables.
Remove onto a serving dish. Mix
the cornflour from the sauce
ingredients with 30ml (2 tblsp)
water. Add the remaining sauce
ingredients to the wok and bring to
the boil. Add the blended
cornflour. Stir and simmer until the
sauce thickens, simmer for 1-2
minutes. Pour over the pork and
serve.

Deep Fried Pork Meat Balls

PREPARATION TIME: 25 minutes

COOKING TIME: about 12
minutes

*450g (1lb) lean pork, coarsely
   minced*
1 small onion, finely chopped
1 green chilli, chopped
*Salt and freshly ground black pepper
   to taste*
*2.5cm (½″) fresh root ginger, peeled
   and finely chopped*
1 egg, beaten
15ml (1 tblsp) cornflour
10ml (2 tsp) dark soya sauce

*2 sprigs Chinese parsley, finely
   chopped*
5ml (1 tsp) cooked oil
Oil for deep frying
*2 spring onions, chopped (for
   garnishing)*
*1 green pepper, seeded and cut into
   rings (for garnishing) (optional)*

Mix the minced pork with the
chopped onion, chilli, salt and
pepper to taste, chopped ginger,
beaten egg, cornflour, soya sauce,
parsley and cooked oil. Leave to
stand for 10 minutes. Mould into
16 even-sized balls. Heat the oil in
the wok for deep frying and slide a
few pork balls into the oil. Fry over
a gentle heat for 5-6 minutes until

**Facing page: Fried Pork with
Vegetables (top left), Bean
Sprouts with Chopped Pork
(centre right) and Deep Fried
Pork Meat Balls (bottom).**

Braised Hong Kong Beef

PREPARATION TIME: 30 minutes

COOKING TIME: about 15-17 minutes

30ml (2 tblsp) oil
450g (1lb) fillet of beef, sliced into matchstick-size strips
1 onion, peeled and sliced
2.5cm (1") fresh root ginger, peeled and cut into thin strips
3-4 fresh tomatoes, cut into thin wedges
225g (½lb) carrots, scraped and cut into 5cm (2") sticks
10ml (2 tsp) brown sugar
2.5ml (½ tsp) five spice powder
30ml (2 tblsp) light soya sauce
15ml (1 tblsp) rice wine or dry sherry
30ml (2 tblsp) water
Salt to taste

Heat the oil in a wok and fry the beef for 3-4 minutes. Add the onion, ginger, tomatoes and carrots. Stir fry for 2-3 minutes. Add the sugar, five spice powder, soya sauce, wine and water. Season with salt to taste and cook gently for 8-10 minutes. Serve as a side dish.

Pork with Green Pepper

PREPARATION TIME: 20 minutes

COOKING TIME: 1 hour 15 minutes

450g (1lb) pork fillet, cut into 5cm (2") strips

Seasoning
1.25ml (¼ tsp) sugar
1.25ml (¼ tsp) monosodium glutamate (optional)
5ml (1 tsp) light soya sauce
10ml (2 tsp) sweet bean paste
10ml (2 tsp) Shao Hsing wine or dry sherry
60ml (4 tblsp) chicken stock

Oil for deep frying
2 cloves garlic, peeled and cut into thin strips
1 green pepper, seeded and sliced into strips
1 green chilli, sliced into strips
1 red chilli, cut in half then sliced into strips

Sauce
5ml (1 tsp) cornflour
15ml (1 tblsp) water

Boil the pork in water for ¾ hour until cooked. Drain the pork and discard the water. Mix the seasoning ingredients together and stir in the pork. Leave to stand for 10 minutes. Heat the wok and add

the oil for deep frying. When oil is very hot fry the drained pork for a few minutes until golden brown. Remove and drain the pork and keep the oil for future use. Reheat the wok and add 5ml (1 tsp) oil and stir fry the garlic for 1 minute. Add the pepper and chillis and stir fry for 1 minute. Add the remaining seasoning mixture and the pork. Stir fry over a gentle heat for 1-2 minutes and then add the blended sauce ingredients. Cook until the sauce thickens. Remove from the heat and serve immediately. Serve with mixed fried rice or rice noodles.

Steamed Pork with Salted Cabbage

PREPARATION TIME: 25 minutes

COOKING TIME: 2 hours

450g (1lb) fillet pork cut into 1cm (½") thick slices
Salt
175g (6oz) cabbage, shredded (Chinese white or plain green cabbage)

Seasoning
15ml (1 tblsp) sugar
30ml (2 tblsp) cooked oil
5ml (1 tsp) monosodium glutamate (optional)
60ml (4 tblsp) stock or water
Salt and freshly ground black pepper

15ml (1 tblsp) dark soya sauce
Oil for deep frying

Sauce
5ml (1 tsp) cornflour
15ml (1 tblsp) water

Boil the pork in 450ml (¾ pint) water for ¾ hour until tender. Drain the pork and discard the water. Boil 450ml (¾ pint) fresh water with 5ml (1 tsp) salt and add the cabbage. Cook for 2 minutes. Drain, rinse in cold water and then drain again. Season the cabbage with 5ml (1 tsp) of the sugar and 15ml (1 tblsp) of the cooked oil. Mix well and keep on one side. Place the pork in a dish and mix with the dark soya sauce. Leave for 10 minutes. Drain. Mix all the seasoning ingredients together. Heat the oil for deep frying and fry the pork until it turns lightly golden. Drain and add to the seasoning mixture. Keep the oil for future use. Place the pork and the seasoning mixture into a deep dish and put the boiled cabbage on top. Cover and steam over boiling water for 1 hour. Drain off any

excess liquid and retain. Heat the wok and add the cabbage liquid. Add the blended sauce thickening of cornflour and water. Stir over the heat until the sauce thickens. Pour over the cabbage and pork and serve.

Bean Sprouts with Chopped Pork

PREPARATION TIME: 15 minutes

COOKING TIME: 10 minutes

225g (½ lb) lean pork, chopped finely or coarsely minced

Marinade
2.5ml (½ tsp) salt
15ml (1 tblsp) light soya sauce
1 egg white, beaten
5ml (1 tsp) cornflour

450g (1lb) bean sprouts
Oil for cooking

Seasoning
2.5ml (½ tsp) salt
2.5ml (½ tsp) sugar
2.5ml (½ tsp) monosodium glutamate (optional)
10ml (2 tsp) soya sauce
5ml (1 tsp) rice wine or dry sherry
15ml (1 tblsp) oyster sauce

2.5cm (½") fresh root ginger, peeled and thinly sliced
2-3 spring onions, chopped
120ml (4 fl oz) chicken stock

Sauce
2.5ml (½ tsp) cornflour or arrowroot
15ml (1 tblsp) water or stock
Few drops of sesame oil

Mix the pork with the marinade ingredients and keep on one side for 10 minutes. Trim the bean sprouts and chop them coarsely. Heat the wok and 30ml (2 tblsp) oil. Stir fry the bean sprouts for 1 minute to evaporate excess water and moisture. Remove the bean sprouts and keep on a plate. Mix the seasoning ingredients together. Heat 45ml (3 tblsp) oil in the wok until it smokes. Stir fry the pork for 2 minutes and then add the ginger, onions and bean sprouts. Stir fry for 2-3 minutes. Add the seasoning ingredients and stir fry for 1 minute. Add the chicken stock and the blended sauce ingredients. Cook until the sauce thickens. Serve immediately.

Spiced Liver (top), Sliced Beef in Oyster Sauce (centre right) and Braised Hong Kong Beef (right).

Oil for frying
1 small onion, peeled and thickly
  sliced
3 spring onions, chopped lengthways
2 leeks, white part only, cut into 4cm
  (1½") slices
5ml (1 tsp) sesame oil

Mix the marinade ingredients with
the beef strips. Leave to marinate
for 20 minutes. Mix all the
seasoning ingredients together in a
small bowl. Heat 30ml (2 tblsp) oil
in a wok and when it is smoking,
add the beef. Reduce the heat and
stir fry for 4-5 minutes. Remove
the meat and keep the oil for future
use. Heat the wok, add 30ml (2
tblsp) fresh oil and stir fry the
onion and leeks for 2 minutes. Add
seasoning mixture and beef and stir
fry for 1-2 minutes. Sprinkle
sesame oil over the top and mix
well. Serve immediately. Use as a
main dish or a side dish.

Shredded Beef with Vegetables

PREPARATION TIME: 15 minutes

COOKING TIME: 10 minutes

225g (8oz) lean beef, cut into thin
  strips
Pinch salt
60ml (4 tblsp) oil
2 red and green chillis, cut in half
  then sliced into strips
5ml (1 tsp) black vinegar
1 stem of celery, cut into 5cm (2")
  thin strips
2 carrots, cut into 5cm (2") thin strips
1 leek, white part only, sliced into
  5cm (2") thin strips
2 cloves of garlic, peeled and finely
  chopped

Seasoning
5ml (1 tsp) light soya sauce
5ml (1 tsp) dark soya sauce
10ml (2 tsp) Shao Hsing wine
5ml (1 tsp) sugar
Pinch monosodium glutamate
  (optional)
2.5ml (½ tsp) freshly ground black
  pepper

**This page: Stir Fried Beef with
Spring Onions (top), Shredded
Beef with Vegetables (centre
left) and Sesame Beef with
Dates (bottom). Facing page:
Beef with Green Beans (top),
Beef Steak with Ginger (centre
right) and Sweet and Sour Beef
(bottom).**

Spiced Liver

PREPARATION TIME: 10 minutes

COOKING TIME: 20 minutes

450g (1lb) lamb's liver, cut into
  2.5cm (1") cubes
120ml (8 tblsp) soya sauce
3-4 spring onions, chopped
30ml (2 tblsp) rice wine or dry sherry
10ml (2 tsp) sugar
2.5cm (1") fresh root ginger, peeled
  and finely chopped
2.5ml (½ tsp) freshly ground black
  pepper
Pinch anise powder

Boil the liver in sufficient water to
just cover, for 3-4 minutes. Drain
well. Add soya sauce, spring
onions, wine, sugar, ginger, pepper
and anise powder. Simmer gently
for 10-15 minutes, covered, until
the liver is tender. Serve as a side
dish.

Stir Fried Beef with Spring Onions

PREPARATION TIME: 30 minutes

COOKING TIME: 10 minutes

Marinade
15ml (1 tblsp) cornflour or arrowroot
1 egg white
15ml (1 tblsp) oil
5ml (1 tsp) bicarbonate of soda
450g (1lb) beef fillet, cut into 2.5cm
  (1") strips

Seasoning
5ml (1 tsp) Shao Hsing wine
15ml (1 tblsp) light soya sauce
5ml (1 tsp) dark soya sauce
2.5ml (½ tsp) salt
2.5ml (½ tsp) freshly ground black
  pepper
5ml (1 tsp) monosodium glutamate
  (optional)

Put the beef into a bowl and sprinkle with salt; rub salt into meat. Heat 5ml (1 tsp) oil in a wok until it begins to smoke. Reduce heat and add beef and chillis and stir fry for 4-5 minutes. Add remaining oil, and stir fry beef until it turns crispy. Add vinegar and mix until it evaporates then add celery, carrots, leeks and garlic. Stir fry for 2 minutes. Mix the seasoning ingredients and pour over the beef and cook for 2 minutes. Serve immediately.

Steamed Lamb with Mushroom Sauce

PREPARATION TIME: 20-25 minutes

COOKING TIME: 2 hours 10 minutes

1kg (2¼lb) boned leg of lamb, cut into 2.5cm (1") cubes
2 onions, thinly sliced
Salt and freshly ground black pepper
10ml (2 tsp) oil
2 cloves of garlic, peeled and sliced

5ml (1 tsp) cornflour
Pinch monosodium glutamate (optional)
75ml (5 tblsp) light soya sauce
45ml (3 tblsp) rice wine or dry sherry
5ml (1 tsp) crushed black pepper
2.5cm (1") fresh root ginger, peeled and thinly sliced
Few drops sesame oil

Put the lamb into a saucepan and add sufficient water to cover. Boil for 5 minutes. Drain the lamb and retain the water. Arrange the lamb cubes in a deep dish and sprinkle the onions on top. Season with pepper and salt. Heat the oil in a wok and fry the garlic until brown. Remove the garlic and discard. Mix together the cornflour, monosodium glutamate, soya sauce, wine, crushed pepper, ginger and 60ml (4 tblsp) reserved water. Stir the cornflour mixture into the oil in the wok and cook for 1-2 minutes. Pour over the lamb. Cover the lamb with overlapping foil and tie around the rim. Put the dish in a steamer and steam over boiling water for 2 hours. Serve with the sesame oil sprinkled over the lamb.

Lamb with Tomatoes

PREPARATION TIME: 20 minutes

COOKING TIME: about 10 minutes

10ml (2 tsp) cornflour
2.5ml (½ tsp) salt
15ml (1 tblsp) light soya sauce
60ml (4 tblsp) water
45ml (3 tblsp) oil
1cm (½") fresh root ginger, sliced
225g (½lb) lamb fillet, cut across the grain in thin strips of 1x5cm (½x2")
2 spring onions, chopped
1 onion, peeled and cut into 2.5cm (1") pieces
1 green pepper, seeded and cut into strips
5ml (1 tsp) curry powder
3-4 small, firm tomatoes, cut into 1cm (½") pieces

Mix the cornflour, salt, soya sauce, water and 5ml (1 tsp) of the oil together. Keep on one side. Heat the remaining oil in a wok and fry the ginger and lamb for 2-3 minutes. Add the onions, green pepper and curry powder and stir fry for 3-4 minutes. Stir in the

cornflour mixture and cook for 1 minute. Add the tomatoes and cook until the sauce thickens. Serve as a side dish.

Mongolian Lamb with Onions

PREPARATION TIME: 20 minutes

COOKING TIME: 8-10 minutes

450g (1lb) lean, boned lamb, cut into 5x50mm (¼x2") strips
1 egg white
2 cloves of garlic, sliced
2.5ml (½ tsp) five spice powder
1cm (½") fresh root ginger, peeled and thinly sliced
15ml (1 tblsp) cornflour
15ml (1 tblsp) light soya sauce
45ml (3 tblsp) rice wine or dry sherry
30ml (2 tblsp) water
45ml (3 tblsp) cooked oil
6 spring onions, chopped

Mix the lamb with the egg white, garlic, five spice powder, ginger root and 5ml (1 tsp) cornflour and 5ml (1 tsp) soya sauce. Keep on one side. Mix the remaining cornflour,

Lamb with Tomatoes (below left), Steamed Lamb with Mushroom Sauce (right) and Mongolian Lamb with Onions (below right).

soya sauce, wine and water together. Heat the wok and add the oil. When it begins to smoke, add the beef mixture. Reduce the heat and stir fry for 3-4 minutes until the meat browns slightly. Remove and keep on one side. Add the onions and the cornflour, soya sauce and wine mixture to the wok. Stir until it thickens. Return the meat to the wok and simmer gently for 3-4 minutes, or until the meat is tender. Serve as a main dish.

Sweet and Sour Beef

PREPARATION TIME: 15 minutes

COOKING TIME: 15 minutes

Batter
100g (4oz) plain flour
7.5ml (1½ tsp) baking powder
60ml (4 tblsp) cornflour
15ml (1 tblsp) oil
45ml (3 tblsp) oil
225g (8oz) fillet of beef, cut into 2.5cm (1") cubes

1 onion, peeled and cut into wedges
2.5cm (1") fresh root ginger, peeled and thinly sliced
1 clove garlic, peeled and thinly sliced
1 green pepper, seeded and chopped

Sweet and Sour Sauce
60ml (4 tblsp) sugar
1.25ml (¼ tsp) salt
60ml (4 tblsp) red or malt vinegar
5ml (1 tsp) fresh root ginger, peeled and minced
90ml (6 tblsp) water

15ml (1 tblsp) cornflour or arrowroot
10ml (2 tsp) cooked oil
Few drops food colouring
Oil for deep frying

For the batter: sieve the flour, baking powder and cornflour. Beat in the oil and add sufficient water to make a thick, smooth batter. Heat the 45ml (3 tblsp) oil in a wok and stir fry the beef for 2 minutes. Remove the beef. Fry the onion, ginger, garlic and green pepper for 2-3 minutes in the same oil. Remove the wok from the heat. Mix the sauce ingredients together and add to the wok. Return the wok to the heat and bring to the boil gently. Lower the heat and simmer gently for 2-3 minutes until thick and clear. Meanwhile, dip the beef cubes into the batter and deep fry in hot oil until golden brown and crisp. Drain on absorbent paper. Arrange in a deep dish and pour the hot sauce over the beef. Serve with a chow mein dish or fried rice. Thinly sliced carrots, cucumber and courgette may also be added along with the onion, ginger and green pepper.

Barbecued Pork
(Kan Hsiang Ch'a Shao or Char Siu)

PREPARATION TIME: 3 hours

COOKING TIME: 1 hour to 1 hour 30 minutes

2kg (4½lb) loin of pork

Seasoning
15ml (1 tblsp) ginger juice
Few drops red food colouring
75ml (5 tblsp) sugar
200ml (⅓ pint) light soya sauce
5ml (1 tsp) salt
15ml (1 tblsp) Mue Kwe Lo wine (or a mixture of 10ml (2 tsp) dry sherry and 5ml (1 tsp) apricot brandy)

225g (½lb) honey, melted

Remove the bones from the loin of pork. Cut pork into 4cm (1½") wide strips. With the aid of a fork scrape the surface of the pork lightly to form grooves in which the seasoning can lodge. Mix the seasoning ingredients together and rub well into the pork strips. Leave to marinate for at least 1½ hours. Thread the pork strips onto a long metal skewer and hang to dry for 1 hour. Put the pork onto a wire rack in a roasting tin. Brush with melted honey and roast in the oven 180°C, 350°F, Gas Mark 4, for 1-1½ hours, basting with honey frequently. When cooked, brush the pork with any remaining honey and leave to 'dry' slightly. Serve hot or cold, sliced thinly on a serving plate.

Pork Spare Ribs

PREPARATION TIME: 25 minutes

COOKING TIME: 40-45 minutes

16-20 spare ribs
5ml (1 tsp) salt
Oil
5ml (1 tsp) ginger paste
5ml (1 tsp) garlic paste

Pork Meat Balls in Sauce (left), Pork Spare Ribs (above) and Barbecued Pork (right).

5ml (1 tsp) onion paste
Pinch monosodium glutamate
  (optional)
5ml (1 tsp) light soya sauce
5ml (1 tsp) cornflour
1 egg
2.5ml (½ tsp) Shao Hsing wine
2.5ml (½ tsp) chilli oil

Sauce
45ml (3 tblsp) sugar
45ml (3 tblsp) black vinegar
15ml (1 tblsp) tomato ketchup
  (optional)
5ml (1 tsp) cornflour
5ml (1 tsp) water
15ml (1 tblsp) dark soya sauce
2.5ml (½ tsp) salt
2.5ml (½ tsp) freshly ground black
  pepper

Trim excess fat from spare ribs and rub with salt. Add 60ml (4 tblsp) oil to the wok and fry the ginger, garlic and onion for 1-2 minutes. Add the spare ribs and stir fry for 6 minutes. Remove to a dish and add the monosodium glutamate, light soya sauce, cornflour, egg, wine and chilli oil. Marinate for 10 minutes. Prepare the sauce by mixing all the ingredients together in the wok and bringing them gently to the boil. Simmer for 2-3 minutes and add the spare ribs along with their marinade. Stir fry until the liquid is

reduced to half its original quantity. Put all the ingredients onto a baking tray and spread out evenly. Bake at 190°C, 375°F, Gas Mark 5, for 25 minutes. Baste occasionally with the liquid from the tray and oil. The spare ribs should have browned well and be well coated with seasoning. Serve hot or cold.

Pork Meat Balls in Sauce
(Sha Kwo Shih-tzu-Tou)

PREPARATION TIME: 25 minutes	
COOKING TIME: 45 minutes	

Seasoning
Pinch monosodium glutamate
  (optional)
15ml (1 tblsp) Shao Hsing wine
2cm (1") fresh root ginger, peeled and
  ground
2 spring onions, white part only,
  minced
2.5ml (½ tsp) salt
10ml (2 tsp) cornflour

450g (1lb) lean pork, minced
25g (1oz) bamboo shoots, chopped
50g (2oz) dried Chinese mushrooms,
  soaked, drained and sliced
1 egg, beaten
Cornflour to roll the meat balls in

175g (6oz) Chinese white cabbage,
  cut into 7.5cm (3") pieces or 225g
  (8oz) ordinary green leafy cabbage,
  cut into 7.5cm (3") pieces
15ml (1 tblsp) cooked oil
Oil for deep frying
15ml (1 tblsp) cornflour
45ml (3 tblsp) water
1 small onion, peeled and finely
  chopped
2.5cm (1") fresh root ginger, peeled
  and finely chopped
300ml (½ pint) chicken stock

Sauce
Salt to taste
2.5ml (½ tsp) monosodium
  glutamate (optional)
15ml (1 tblsp) light soya sauce
5ml (1 tsp) dark soya sauce
15ml (1 tblsp) cooked oil

Mix seasoning ingredients together. Add the pork, bamboo shoots, mushrooms and egg and mix well. Shape into 15-16 even-sized balls and roll them in cornflour. Keep aside on a dish. Blanch cabbage for 1 minute in boiling water and the cooked oil. Drain the cabbage and discard the water. Heat the wok and add the oil for deep frying. When quite hot deep-fry the meat balls, a few at a time, for 4-5 minutes. Remove and drain. Keep warm in a large casserole dish.

Keep oil for future use. Mix the 15ml (1 tblsp) cornflour with the 45ml (3 tblsp) water and keep aside. Reheat the wok and add 5ml (1 tsp) deep frying oil. Stir fry the onion and ginger for 2 minutes. Add the chicken stock and stir in the blended sauce ingredients. Bring to the boil and add the meat balls. Simmer gently for 30 minutes. Add the cabbage, sesame oil and the blended cornflour mixture. Stir over the heat until the sauce thickens.

Sesame Beef with Dates

PREPARATION TIME: 20 minutes, plus 30 minutes to marinate

COOKING TIME: 12-15 minutes

Seasoning A
2.5ml (½ tsp) bicarbonate of soda
15ml (1 tblsp) light soya sauce
15ml (1 tblsp) oil
7.5ml (1½ tsp) cornflour
450g (1lb) beef fillet, thinly sliced into 5cm (2") pieces
20 dried dates (red or dark), soaked and stoned

Seasoning B
5ml (1 tsp) monosodium glutamate (optional)
7.5ml (1½ tsp) sugar
10ml (2 tsp) bean paste
200ml (⅓ pint) beef stock, or made with stock cube
Salt to taste
60ml (4 tblsp) cooked oil or plain oil
2.5cm (1") fresh root ginger, peeled and thinly sliced
2 spring onions, sliced

Sauce
15ml (1 tblsp) cornflour
30ml (2 tblsp) water or stock
30ml (2 tblsp) sesame seeds

Mix the ingredients for seasoning A. Mix with the beef and marinate for 30 minutes. Drain meat and discard marinade. Drain soaked dates; slice most of them into 4 long pieces, leaving a few whole. Mix the dates with seasoning B. Heat oil in a wok and stir fry beef for 4-5 minutes. Add ginger, spring onions, dates and the seasoning B and gently bring to the boil. Add the blended sauce ingredients. Cover and simmer for 3-4 minutes over a gentle heat until the sauce thickens and becomes clear. Remove from the heat, place on a serving dish and keep warm. Heat a wok or frying pan and add the sesame seeds. Dry roast for 2

minutes until they begin to crackle and turn golden brown. Sprinkle over the beef and serve immediately.

Shredded Pork with Preserved Vegetables

PREPARATION TIME: 30 minutes

COOKING TIME: 6-8 minutes

Pinch monosodium glutamate (optional)
10ml (2 tsp) cornflour
Salt and freshly ground black pepper to taste
225g (½ lb) lean pork, shredded
Oil
2.5cm (1") fresh root ginger, peeled and shredded
50g (2oz) shelled green peas
2.5ml (½ tsp) sugar
10ml (2 tsp) Shao Hsing wine or dry sherry
225g (8oz) Shanghai preserved vegetables (mixed), in brine
5ml (1 tsp) sesame oil

Mix the monosodium glutamate, cornflour and a pinch of salt. Add the pork and let it stand for 15 minutes. Heat the oil in a wok and deep fry the pork for 3 minutes. Remove the pork and drain. Reserve oil for future use. Reheat wok and add 10ml (2 tsp) deep fried oil. Stir fry the ginger and green peas for 1 minute. Add the pork and sprinkle with the sugar, wine and salt and pepper to taste. Stir fry for another minute and add the well-drained, preserved vegetables. Allow to heat through and then stir gently. Sprinkle on the sesame oil and serve. Serve as a side dish or on a bed of plain fried noodles.

Beef Steak with Ginger

PREPARATION TIME: 20-25 minutes

COOKING TIME: 10-12 minutes

Seasoning
2.5ml (½ tsp) bicarbonate of soda
45ml (3 tblsp) light soya sauce
30ml (2 tblsp) rice wine or dry sherry
2.5ml (½ tsp) salt
2.5ml (½ tsp) ground black pepper
1.25cm (½ tsp) fresh root ginger, peeled and minced
225g (½lb) beef fillet, sliced into 2.5cm (1") pieces

Sauce
5ml (1 tsp) sugar
1.25ml (¼ tsp) monosodium glutamate (optional)
15ml (1 tblsp) dark soya sauce
45ml (3 tblsp) stock
Few drops sesame oil
5ml (1 tsp) Shao Hsing wine
60ml (4 tblsp) oil
2.5cm (1") fresh root ginger, peeled and thinly sliced
4 spring onions, chopped
50g (2oz) bamboo shoots, thinly sliced
2 green chillis, sliced

Mix the seasoning ingredients with the minced ginger. Add the beef and marinate for 20 minutes. Drain the beef and discard the marinade. Mix the sauce ingredients together. Heat 45ml (3 tblsp) oil in the wok and fry the sliced ginger and onions for 2 minutes. Add the bamboo shoots and chillis and stir fry for 1-2 minutes. Remove to a plate. Add the remaining oil to the wok and fry the beef for 2-3 minutes. Add fried vegetables and stir fry for 2 minutes. Add well-stirred sauce ingredients and simmer gently until the mixture thickens. Simmer for another 1-2 minutes. Remove from heat and serve.

Beef with Green Beans

PREPARATION TIME: 30 minutes

COOKING TIME: 12 minutes

Seasoning
2.5ml (½ tsp) bicarbonate of soda
5ml (1 tsp) cornflour
15ml (1 tblsp) light soya sauce
30ml (2 tblsp) water
5ml (1 tsp) cooked oil
450g (1lb) lean beef, thinly sliced into 2.5cm (1") pieces

Sauce
1.25ml (¼ tsp) salt
5ml (1 tsp) monosodium glutamate (optional)
5ml (1 tsp) light soya sauce
5ml (1 tsp) dark soya sauce
5ml (1 tsp) Shao Hsing wine (optional)
120ml (4 fl oz) stock
10ml (2 tsp) cornflour
45ml (3 tblsp) oil
2 cloves of garlic, peeled and sliced
1 onion, peeled and cut into wedges
2.5cm (1") fresh ginger root, peeled and sliced thinly
175g (6oz) Chinese long beans, cut into 7.5cm (3") pieces, or whole tender green beans
Salt and freshly ground black pepper to taste

Mix seasoning ingredients together. Add the beef and marinate for 20 minutes. Drain the meat and discard the marinade. Mix the sauce ingredients together. Heat 30ml (2 tblsp) oil in the wok until it smokes. Reduce the heat add the garlic and the beef, and stir fry for 3-4 minutes. Remove the meat and keep on one side. Add the remaining oil to the wok and add the onion, ginger and long beans and stir fry for 2-3 minutes. Add fried beef. Cover and fry for a further 1 minute. Stir in the sauce ingredients and bring to the boil. Simmer gently for 2-3 minutes. Season with salt and pepper. Remove from heat and serve.

Sweet and Sour Pork

PREPARATION TIME: 20 minutes, plus 20 minutes to marinate

COOKING TIME: 15-20 minutes

Batter
45ml (3 tblsp) flour
15ml (1 tblsp) cornflour
7.5ml (1½ tsp) bicarbonate of soda
30ml (2 tblsp) oil

350g (12oz) lean pork, cut into 2.5cm (1") cubes

Seasoning
5ml (1 tsp) sugar
5ml (1 tsp) salt
30ml (2 tblsp) light soya sauce
5ml (1 tsp) dark soya sauce
15ml (1 tblsp) cooked oil
15ml (1 tblsp) water

Cornflour
Oil for deep frying
2 cloves garlic, cut into thin strips
1 large onion, peeled and cut into 1cm (½") pieces
1 carrot, sliced into 3x25x50mm (⅛x1x2") thin pieces
Pinch salt

Sweet and Sour Sauce
45ml (3 tblsp) sugar
15ml (1 tblsp) tomato purée
250ml (8 fl oz) chicken stock or water
60ml (4 tblsp) red or white vinegar
5ml (1 tsp) light soya sauce
Few slices fresh root ginger, peeled
15ml (1 tblsp) cornflour or arrowroot
Few drops of red food colouring
10ml (2 tsp) cooked oil

Mix the batter ingredients together, adding sufficient water to make a thick coating batter. Wash and drain the pork. Mix with the seasoning ingredients and marinate

Seasoning

7.5ml (1½ tsp) light soya sauce
Few drops sesame oil
Salt and freshly ground black pepper
* to taste*
15ml (1 tblsp) oil
15ml (1 tblsp) water
15ml (1 tblsp) cornflour
Pinch monosodium glutamate
* (optional)*

225g (½ lb) pork fillet, cut into cubes
1 carrot, thinly sliced
1 onion, peeled and cut into pieces
3 spring onions, chopped
2.5cm (1″) fresh root ginger, peeled
* and thinly sliced*

Sauce

90ml (6 tblsp) stock
5ml (1 tsp) cornflour

Cook the walnuts in boiling water for 3-4 minutes. Drain the nuts thoroughly. Deep fry the walnuts until lightly browned. Remove and drain. Use oil for cooking. Mix the seasoning ingredients together and add the pork. Leave to marinate for 15 minutes. Discard marinade. Heat 30ml (2 tblsp) oil in the wok and stir-fry the carrots for 2 minutes. Add the onions and root ginger and stir fry for 1 minute. Add 10ml (2 tsp) of the sauce stock and remove to a plate. Add the drained pork cubes and 15ml (1 tblsp) oil to the wok and stir fry for 4-5 minutes. Mix the remaining stock and the cornflour together for the sauce. Return the walnuts and carrots to the wok, together with the blended sauce ingredients. Mix well and simmer until the sauce thickens. Remove and serve immediately. Serve with rice noodles or fried rice.

for 15-20 minutes. Drain the pork and discard the marinade. Roll the pork cubes in cornflour. Heat the oil for deep frying. Dip the pork cubes in batter and fry in the hot oil until golden brown. Fry a few at a time until all the pork has been fried. Drain well and keep warm in a low oven. Heat wok and add 10ml (2 tsp) deep fried oil. Stir fry

the garlic, onions and carrots for 3-4 minutes. Season with salt and fry for a further minute. Mix the sweet and sour sauce ingredients together and add to the wok. Stir the mixture until it thickens. Pour over the fried pork cubes and serve immediately. Note: sliced green peppers can also be added along with the carrots and onions.

Diced Pork with Walnuts

PREPARATION TIME: 30 minutes

COOKING TIME: 16-18 minutes

100g (4oz) shelled walnuts
Oil for deep frying

Sweet and Sour Pork (top right), Diced Pork with Walnuts (centre) and Shredded Pork with Preserved Vegetables (bottom left).

Poultry

Roast Crispy Duck

PREPARATION TIME: 15-20
minutes plus 6-8 hours to dry

COOKING TIME: 1 hour
30 minutes

*2kg (4½lb) duck or goose, prepared
for cooking
250ml (8 fl oz) water
6 large scallions or 12 spring onions,
cut into 5cm (2 inch) lengths
60ml (4 tblsp) maltose or golden
syrup
2.5ml (½ tsp) red food colouring
30ml (2 tblsp) tomato purée*

Wash the duck and pat it dry on a
clean cloth. Ease the fingers
between the skin and flesh of the
duck, starting at the neck end and
working the length of the bird. Put
a stick or large skewer through the
neck and the cavity of the duck to
wedge it securely. This will make
the duck easier to handle. Hold the
duck over the sink and pour
boiling water all over it. Pat the
duck dry. Melt half the maltose and
dissolve in the water. Stand the
duck on a rack over a deep tray.
Slowly pour the maltose liquid
over the duck. Pour the maltose
liquid over the duck 3 or 4 times.
Leave the duck in a cool place for
6-8 hours, or overnight, until the
skin is dry. Remove the stick. Stand
the duck on a rack in a roasting tin.
Preheat the oven to 200°C, 400°F,
Gas Mark 6 and cook for 30
minutes. Turn over and cook the
underside for a further 30 minutes.
Melt the remaining maltose with
the tomato purée and add the food
colouring. Spread over the duck
and cook for a further 30 minutes.
(The duck should have a crisp, red
skin.) Remove the duck skin in
squares. Slice the duck flesh and
serve with the skin on the top.
Serve the following dip as an
accompaniment.

Duck Dip
*100g (4oz) sugar
60ml (4 tblsp) sweet bean paste
30ml (2 tblsp) sesame oil
120ml (4 fl oz) water*

Heat the wok and add the mixed
ingredients. Cook for 3-4 minutes
until the sugar has dissolved and
the dip is smooth. Serve in
individual cups.

Sliced Duck with Bamboo Shoots

PREPARATION TIME: 30 minutes

COOKING TIME: 10 minutes

*1kg (2¼lb) small duck
5ml (1 tsp) monosodium glutamate
(optional)
12.5ml (2½ tsp) cornflour
30ml (2 tblsp) water
100g (4oz) broccoli, chopped
45ml (3 tblsp) oil
2-3 spring onions, chopped
2.5cm (1 inch) fresh root ginger,
peeled and thinly sliced
1 clove garlic, peeled and finely
chopped
100g (4oz) bamboo shoots, sliced
2.5ml (½ tsp) sugar
Salt and freshly ground black pepper
to taste
60ml (4 tblsp) chicken stock
10ml (2 tsp) rice wine or sweet sherry
Few drops sesame oil*

Cut the duck flesh into bite-size
pieces, removing all the bones. Mix

the MSG, 7.5ml (1½ tsp)
cornflour and 15ml (1 tblsp) water
together. Stir into the duck.
Marinate for 20 minutes. Cook the
broccoli in boiling water for 1
minute. Drain thoroughly. Heat the
wok and add the oil. Stir fry the
onions, ginger, garlic and bamboo
shoots for 1-2 minutes. Add the
duck pieces and stir fry for 2-3
minutes. Add the sugar, salt and
pepper to taste, stock, rice wine
and sesame oil. Stir fry for 3
minutes. Add the remaining
cornflour and water blended
together. Stir over the heat until
the sauce thickens. Serve
immediately, as a side dish.

Duck with Ginger and Pineapple

PREPARATION TIME: 20 minutes

COOKING TIME: 2 hours to 2
hours 45 minutes

*1.25cm (½ inch) fresh root ginger,
peeled and crushed
2kg (4½lb) duck
Salt and freshly ground black pepper
to taste
45ml (3 tblsp) oil
10cm (4 inches) fresh root ginger,
peeled and thinly sliced
50g (2oz) bean sprouts
3 spring onions, chopped
2 carrots, peeled, sliced and blanched
in boiling water for 2 minutes
10ml (2 tsp) brown sugar
15ml (1 tblsp) wine vinegar
5ml (1 tsp) white vinegar
225g (8oz) can pineapple chunks in
syrup
15ml (1 tblsp) cornflour mixed with
30ml (2 tblsp) water*

Mix together the crushed ginger,
half of the soya sauce and salt and
pepper to taste. Wash the duck and
pat it dry. Rub the outside of the
duck with salt and put on a wire
rack in a roasting tin. Roast at
180°C, 350°F, Gas Mark 4, for 30
minutes. Brush the ginger and soya
sauce mixture over the duck. Baste
frequently with the sauces from the
pan and roast for 2 hours, turning
the bird occasionally to brown all
sides. Remove and slice the duck in
small pieces. Heat the oil in a wok
and stir fry the sliced ginger, bean
sprouts, onions and carrots for 1-2
minutes. Add the duck slices and
cook for 1 minute. Then add the
brown sugar, vinegar and pineapple
chunks in their syrup. Bring to the
boil and cook for 2-3 minutes. Add
the blended cornflour and cook
until the sauce thickens. Serve as a
main dish along with noodles or
rice.

**This page: Stewed Chicken and
Pineapple (top right), Fried
Shredded Chicken on Cabbage
(centre left) and Chicken and
Cashew Nuts (bottom right).**

**Facing page: Sliced Duck with
Bamboo Shoots (top), Duck
with Ginger and Pineapple
(bottom left) and Roast Crispy
Duck (bottom right).**

Chicken Green Chilli

PREPARATION TIME: 10 minutes, plus 10 minutes to marinate

COOKING TIME: 10 minutes

Sauce
5ml (1 tsp) light soya sauce
5ml (1 tsp) dark soya sauce
Salt to taste
10ml (2 tsp) cornflour
5ml (1 tsp) sesame oil
5ml (1 tsp) malt vinegar
250ml (8 fl oz) chicken stock

Seasoning
Salt to taste
Freshly ground black pepper to taste
Pinch monosodium glutamate (optional)
30ml (2 tblsp) dark soya sauce
15ml (1 tblsp) light soya sauce
5ml (1 tsp) cornflour
10ml (2 tsp) rice wine or dry sherry

450g (1lb) boned chicken, cut into bite-size pieces
45ml (3 tblsp) oil
3 spring onions, chopped
2.5cm (1") fresh root ginger, peeled and sliced
2 cloves of garlic, peeled and sliced
1 green pepper, seeded and chopped
2-3 green chillis, sliced lengthways

Mix the sauce ingredients together. Mix the seasoning ingredients together and add the chicken. Marinate for 10 minutes. Drain the chicken and discard the liquid. Heat 15ml (1 tblsp) oil and stir fry the onions, ginger and garlic for 2 minutes. Remove to a dish. Add the remaining oil and stir fry the chicken for 3 minutes. Add the blended green peppers and chillis and stir fry for 2 minutes. Add the onion mixture and the well-blended sauce ingredients and cook for 3-4 minutes until the sauce thickens. Serve immediately.

Chicken and Mushrooms

PREPARATION TIME: 15 minutes, plus 10 minutes to marinate

COOKING TIME: 10-12 minutes

Seasoning
2.5ml (1/2 tsp) salt
30ml (2 tblsp) light soya sauce
10ml (2 tsp) cornflour
5ml (1 tsp) rice wine or dry sherry
Pinch monosodium glutamate (optional)

225g (1/2lb) chicken breast, cut into bite-size pieces

Sauce
Salt to taste
Freshly ground black pepper to taste
15ml (1 tblsp) light soya sauce
250ml (8 fl oz) chicken stock
10ml (2 tsp) cornflour or arrowroot
5ml (1 tsp) oyster sauce
30ml (2 tblsp) oil

1 onion, peeled and chopped
1 clove of garlic, sliced
1cm (1/2") fresh root ginger, peeled and thinly sliced
3 dried black mushrooms, soaked and sliced
50g (2oz) open mushrooms, sliced
50g (2oz) button mushrooms, sliced

Mix the seasoning ingredients together. Marinate the chicken in the seasoning mixture for 10 minutes. Mix the sauce ingredients together. Heat the oil in a wok and fry the onion, garlic and ginger for 2-3 minutes. Remove and keep on one side. Fry the drained chicken in the remaining oil for 4 minutes. Add the mushrooms and stir fry for 1 minute. Add a little extra oil if necessary. Return the fried onion mixture to the wok and stir fry until well mixed. Pour the blended sauce ingredients into the wok and cook gently until the sauce thickens. Serve piping hot.

Chicken Fry with Sauce (below right), Chicken Green Chilli (below centre) and Chicken and Mushrooms (far right).

Chicken Fry with Sauce

PREPARATION TIME: 20 minutes
COOKING TIME: about 24 minutes

15ml (1 tblsp) cooked oil
5ml (1 tsp) sesame oil
25g (1oz) sesame seeds

Sauce

2 cloves of garlic, minced
2 spring onions, finely chopped or minced
5ml (1 tsp) Chinese black vinegar or brown malt vinegar
45ml (3 tblsp) dark soya sauce
5ml (1 tsp) light soya sauce
2.5ml (½ tsp) monosodium glutamate (optional)
2.5ml (½ tsp) salt
7.5ml (1½ tsp) sugar
·8 chicken thighs, or 450g (1lb) chicken, cut into small joints

Heat the wok and add the oils. Stir fry the sesame seeds till they change colour to golden brown. Remove onto a dish. Mix sauce ingredients together and add the sesame seeds. Wipe the wok and add the chicken. Add sufficient water to cover, and cook for 20 minutes until the chicken is tender. De-bone the chicken and quickly cut into bite-size pieces. Arrange the chicken on a plate and spoon the sauce over the top. Serve immediately.

Stewed Chicken and Pineapple

PREPARATION TIME: 30 minutes
COOKING TIME: 15 minutes

Seasoning

30ml (2 tblsp) light soya sauce
15ml (1 tblsp) oil
15ml (1 tblsp) cornflour
5ml (1 tsp) salt
2.5ml (½ tsp) sesame oil
30ml (2 tblsp) water
750g (1½lb) boned chicken breast, cut into cubes

Sauce

7.5ml (1½ tsp) cornflour
250ml (8 fl oz) water or chicken stock
10ml (2 tsp) dark soya sauce
Salt to taste
30ml (2 tblsp) oil
1 onion, peeled and cut into chunks
2 spring onions, finely chopped
2.5cm (1") fresh root ginger, peeled and thinly sliced
4-5 pineapple rings, cut into chunks

Mix the seasoning ingredients together. Add the cubed chicken and marinate for 10-12 minutes. Mix the sauce ingredients together in a bowl. Heat the oil in a wok and fry the onions for 2 minutes until just tender. Add the drained chicken and fry for 3-4 minutes. Add the root ginger and fry for 1 minute. Add any remaining marinade and the sauce ingredients

and bring to the boil. Cook, stirring, until the sauce thickens then add the pineapple chunks. Heat through. Remove from the heat and serve with fried rice.

Chicken Chop Suey

PREPARATION TIME: 30 minutes
COOKING TIME: 15 minutes

30ml (2 tblsp) light soya sauce
5ml (1 tsp) brown sugar
Salt to taste
450g (1lb) boned chicken, cut into 2.5cm (1″) pieces
30ml (2 tblsp) cooking oil
1 onion, cut into chunks
225g (8oz) bean sprouts
10ml (2 tsp) sesame oil
1.25g (¼ tsp) monosodium glutamate (optional)
15ml (1 tblsp) cornflour
250ml (8 fl oz) chicken stock

Mix the soya sauce with the sugar and salt and add the chicken pieces. Allow to marinate for 5 minutes. Drain the chicken and reserve the marinade. Heat the wok and add the oil. Fry the chicken for 2-3 minutes. Remove the chicken. Fry the onions for 2-3 minutes and add the beansprouts. Stir fry for 4-5 minutes. Return the chicken to the pan and add the sesame oil. Dissolve the monosodium glutamate and the cornflour in the stock and pour over the chicken mixture. Cook for 2-3 minutes, stirring, until the sauce thickens. Serve as a side dish.

Deep Fried Crispy Chicken

PREPARATION TIME: 3 hours
COOKING TIME: 13-14 minutes

1.5kg (3-3½lb) chicken, prepared for cooking

Seasoning
5ml (1 tsp) salt
2.5ml (½ tsp) five spice powder
40g (1½oz) maltose
30ml (2 tblsp) malt vinegar
150ml (¼ pint) white vinegar
Oil for deep frying

Wash the chicken and hang it up by a hook to drain and dry. The skin will dry quickly. Pour boiling water over the chicken 4-5 times, to partially cook the skin. This will

make the skin crisp during frying. Rub salt and five spice powder well inside the chicken cavity. Dissolve the maltose and vinegars in a pan over a gentle heat. Pour over the chicken. Repeat several times, catching the maltose solution in a drip tray. Leave the chicken to hang and dry for 1½-2 hours, until the skin is smooth and shiny. Heat the oil for deep frying. Deep fry the chicken for 10 minutes. Ladle hot oil carefully over the chicken continually, until the chicken is deep brown in colour. (The skin puffs out slightly.) Cook for a further 3-4 minutes and remove from the oil. Drain on absorbent paper. Cut into small pieces and serve with a dip.

Chicken and Cashew Nuts

PREPARATION TIME: 15 minutes
COOKING TIME: 15 minutes

350g (12oz) chicken breast, sliced into 2.5cm (1″) pieces
15ml (1 tblsp) cornflour

Seasoning
5ml (1 tsp) salt
5ml (1 tsp) sesame oil
15ml (1 tblsp) light soya sauce
2.5ml (½ tsp) sugar
Oil for deep frying
100g (4oz) cashew nuts
2 spring onions, chopped
1 small onion, peeled and cubed
2.5cm (1″) fresh root ginger, peeled and sliced
2 cloves of garlic, sliced
75g (3oz) snow peas (mange tout)
50g (2oz) bamboo shoots, thinly sliced

Sauce
10ml (2 tsp) cornflour
15ml (1 tblsp) Hoi Sin sauce
250ml (just over ⅓ pint) chicken stock
Pinch monosodium glutamate (optional)

Roll the chicken pieces in cornflour. Discard the remaining cornflour. Mix the seasoning ingredients together and pour over chicken. Leave to stand for 10 minutes. Heat oil for deep frying and fry cashew nuts until golden brown. Remove the nuts and drain on kitchen paper. Heat 30ml (2 tblsp) oil in a wok and stir fry the onions, ginger and garlic for 2-3 minutes. Add snow peas and

bamboo shoots and stir fry for 3 minutes. Remove the fried ingredients. Add 15ml (1 tblsp) oil to the wok and fry the chicken for 3-4 minutes. Remove the chicken. Clean the wok and add a further 10ml (2 tblsp) oil and return chicken, cashew nuts and fried onions etc. to the wok. Prepare the sauce by mixing the cornflour, Hoi Sin sauce, chicken stock and monosodium glutamate together. Pour over the chicken. Mix well and cook until the sauce thickens and becomes transparent. Serve hot with a chow mein dish. Alternatively, a few chunks of pineapple will add extra zest to the dish.

Fried Shredded Chicken on Cabbage

PREPARATION TIME: 20 minutes
COOKING TIME: 12 minutes

450g (1lb) Chinese white cabbage, cut into 2.5cm (1″) pieces
Pinch bicarbonate of soda

Seasoning
15ml (1 tblsp) light soya sauce
15ml (1 tblsp) cornflour
1.25ml (¼ tsp) sesame oil
1.25ml (¼ tsp) freshly ground black pepper
2.5ml (½ tsp) sugar
2.5ml (½ tsp) salt
15ml (1 tblsp) water
15ml (1 tblsp) oil
Pinch monosodium glutamate (optional)
30ml (2 tblsp) oil
1 onion, peeled and roughly chopped
2.5cm (1″) fresh root ginger, peeled and thinly sliced
450g (1lb) boned chicken breasts, shredded
4-6 mushrooms, sliced

Sauce
45ml (3 tblsp) chicken stock
1.25ml (¼ tsp) sesame oil
5ml (1 tsp) light soya sauce
5ml (1 tsp) cornflour
5ml (1 tsp) monosodium glutamate (optional)

Wash cabbage and blanch in boiling water with a pinch of bicarbonate of soda for 2 minutes. Drain well. Mix the seasoning ingredients together. Heat the wok and add the oil. Fry the onions, ginger and chicken for 2-3 minutes. Add the mushrooms and fry for further 2 minutes. Add the stock and cook for 4-5 minutes. Mix the

sauce ingredients together and pour over the chicken. Cook for 2 minutes. Serve immediately.

Steamed Chicken

PREPARATION TIME: 20-30 minutes
COOKING TIME: 15-20 minutes

750g (1½lb) boned chicken

Seasoning
15ml (1 tblsp) light soya sauce
5ml (1 tsp) brown sugar
5ml (1 tsp) salt
15ml (1 tblsp) cornflour
30ml (2 tblsp) oil or cooked oil
2.5ml (½ tsp) monosodium glutamate (optional)
100g (4oz) dried mushrooms, soaked in boiling water for 5 minutes and sliced, or ordinary mushrooms
1cm (½″) fresh root ginger, peeled and sliced
4 spring onions, finely chopped
30ml (2 tblsp) stock or water, if needed

Cut the chicken into 2.5cm (1″) pieces. Mix the seasoning ingredients together and mix with the chicken. Leave to marinate for 15 minutes. Place a plate in a steamer and put the chicken, mushrooms, ginger, half the onion and the stock on top. Steam over boiling water for 15-20 minutes. Serve with the remaining onions sprinkled over the chicken. The steaming can also be done on a greased lotus leaf or a banana leaf. The flavour is quite stunning.

Tangerine Peel Chicken

PREPARATION TIME: 30 minutes
COOKING TIME: 12-15 minutes

450g (1lb) boned chicken breast, cut into 2.5cm (1″) pieces

Facing page: Chicken Chop Suey (top left), Steamed Chicken (centre right) and Deep Fried Crispy Chicken (bottom left).

Seasoning
2.5ml (½ tsp) salt
7.5ml (1½ tsp) sugar
2.5ml (½ tsp) monosodium
  glutamate (optional)
5ml (1 tsp) dark soya sauce
10ml (2 tsp) light soya sauce
5ml (1 tsp) rice wine or dry sherry
10ml (2 tsp) malt vinegar
5ml (1 tsp) sesame oil
10ml (2 tsp) cornflour

Oil for deep frying
1-2 red or green chillis, chopped
1.25cm (½") fresh root ginger, peeled
  and finely chopped
5cm (2") dried tangerine peel,
  coarsely ground or crumbled
2 spring onions, finely chopped
Sauce
2.5ml (½ tsp) cornflour
15-30ml (1-2 tblsp) water or stock

Mix the chicken pieces with the
seasoning ingredients and stir well.
Leave to marinate for 10-15
minutes. Remove the chicken
pieces and reserve the marinade.
Heat wok and add the oil for deep
frying. Once it starts to smoke add
the chicken pieces and fry for 4-5
minutes until golden. Drain
chicken on kitchen paper. Tip off
the oil, leaving 15ml (1 tblsp) oil in
the wok, and stir fry the chillis,
ginger, tangerine peel and onions
for 2-3 minutes. When they begin
to colour add the chicken and stir
fry for 1 minute. Mix the reserved
marinade with the sauce
ingredients and pour over the
chicken. Stir and cook for 2-3
minutes until the sauce thickens
and the chicken is tender. Serve
immediately.

Roast Spiced Duck

PREPARATION TIME: 3-4 hours
to dry, and 1 hour to glaze
COOKING TIME: 1 hour

2kg (4½lb) duck or small goose
5ml (1 tsp) five spice powder
7.5ml (1½ tsp) salt
60ml (4 tblsp) maltose or golden
  syrup
5ml (1 tsp) white vinegar
10ml (2 tsp) malt or red vinegar
Oil

Wash and dry the duck. Rub in the
five spice powder and salt. Close
the cavities of the duck by securing
both ends with small skewers. Mix
the maltose and vinegar together
with a little water and bring to the
boil. Spoon this liquid over the
duck several times, collecting the
liquid in a tray. Hang the duck by
its neck for 3-4 hours to dry.

Preheat the oven to 230°C, 450°F,
Gas Mark 8. Place the duck in a
roasting tin. Rub oil into the skin.
Roast in the oven for 1 hour,
basting with any remaining maltose
and vinegar liquid. If the duck is
not quite tender, cook for a little
longer. Slice the duck onto a
warmed serving dish and serve
immediately.

Roast Peking Duck

PREPARATION TIME: 15 minutes
plus 2-3 hours to dry out the skin
COOKING TIME: 1 hour
                   20 minutes

2kg (4½lb) duck or small goose
1 litre (1¾ pints) boiling water
30ml (2 tblsp) maltose or golden
  syrup
250ml (8 fl oz) water
2-3 seedless oranges, peeled and cut
  into rings
30ml (2 tblsp) oil
Salt and freshly ground black pepper

Sauce
10ml (2 tsp) cornflour
60ml (4 tblsp) water or stock
Pinch monosodium glutamate
  (optional)
10ml (2 tsp) light soya sauce
5ml (1 tsp) rice wine or dry sherry

To Garnish
4 spring onions, cut into 5cm (2 inch)
  lengths

Wash and dry the duck. Put a stick
or skewer through the neck and
the cavity of the duck so that it is
easier to handle. Hold the bird
over the sink and pour the boiling
water over it. Hang the duck up to
dry. Melt the maltose and water
together and spoon over the duck
several times, catching the liquid
on a drip tray each time. Leave the
duck to dry for 2-3 hours in a cool
place. Save any liquid that drops
off. Preheat the oven to 200°C,
400°F, Gas Mark 6. Place the duck,
breast side down, in a roasting tin
and roast for 30 minutes. Lift out
the duck. Put the orange rings into
the tin and sit the duck on top,
breast side uppermost. Baste with
the oil and season with salt and
pepper. Roast for a further 45-50
minutes until tender. Cut off the
duck joints and slice the breast
meat. Arrange with the orange
slices on a serving dish and keep
warm.

To Make the Sauce
Mix the sauce ingredients together
and add any reserved maltose
liquid. Bring to the boil gently,

stirring, until the sauce thickens.
Pour over the cooked duck and
sprinkle with the onions. This is
served either as a main dish or as a
side dish.

Steamed Duck in Wine Sauce

PREPARATION TIME: 20 minutes
COOKING TIME: 30 hours
                   30 minutes

2kg (4½lb) duck
150ml (¼ pint) Kao Liang wine or
  mild red wine
2.5ml (½ tsp) monosodium
  glutamate (optional)

**Roast Spiced Duck (top), Roast
Peking Duck (above) and
Steamed Duck in Wine Sauce
(right).**

2.5cm (1 inch) fresh root ginger,
 peeled and thinly sliced
3 spring onions, chopped
5ml (1 tsp) salt
5ml (1 tsp) sugar
5ml (1 tsp) cornflour

Place the duck in a large pot. Add water to cover and boil for 5-7 minutes. Remove the duck and drain well. Mix all the remaining ingredients together apart from the cornflour. Place the duck in a deep dish and stand over a steamer. Pour the wine mixture over the duck. Cover and steam for 2-3 hours until the duck is quite tender. Remove the duck and strain the cooking liquid. Place the duck on a serving dish, either whole or cut into slices. Blend the cooking liquid with the cornflour. Bring to the boil and stir until thickened. Pour over the duck. Serve immediately.

Chicken Chow Mein

PREPARATION TIME: 30 minutes

COOKING TIME: 20 minutes

450g (1lb) egg noodles or spaghetti,
 broken into small pieces
1 onion, peeled and thinly sliced
50g (2oz) mushrooms, sliced
3 spring onions, chopped
2 cloves of garlic, peeled and chopped
Salt to taste
Pinch monosodium glutamate
60ml (4 tblsp) oil
175g (6oz) chicken meat, finely
 shredded
30ml (2 tblsp) light soya sauce
5ml (1 tsp) sugar
15ml (1 tblsp) rice wine or dry sherry
90ml (6 tblsp) chicken stock

Cook the noodles in boiling, salted water for 4-5 minutes until tender. Drain and rinse under cold water. Drain once again and add 30ml (2 tblsp) oil; mix well to prevent the noodles from sticking together. Heat 30ml (2 tblsp) oil in a wok and fry the onions and garlic for 2 minutes. Add chicken and stir fry for 3-4 minutes. Add mushrooms. Sprinkle over the wine, sugar, soya sauce, monosodium glutamate and salt to taste. Cook until the mixture is fairly dry. Add noodles and stir well to mix. Sprinkle over the stock and cook once again until dry. Serve with chilli sauce and dark soya sauce. 50g (2oz) sliced green beans, 50g (2oz) peas or 50g (2oz) shredded carrot may also be added, along with the chicken pieces.

Peking Duck with Pancakes

PREPARATION TIME: for duck 2-3 hours; for pancakes 6 minutes

COOKING TIME: for duck 1 hour 20 minutes; for pancakes 15 minutes

2kg (4½lb) Peking duck, roasted
16-20 spring onions, sliced into
 7.5cm (3 inch) pieces

Pancakes (Po Ping)
450g (1lb) flour
Pinch salt
15ml (1 tblsp) corn oil
5ml (1 tsp) sesame oil
Tepid water for kneading
Flour for rolling

To Make Pancakes
Sift the flour and salt into a mixing bowl. Make a well in the centre and add the corn oil and water, a little at a time, and work in the flour. Make a pliable dough. Remove from the bowl and knead well for 2-3 minutes. Cover with a damp,

clean cloth and allow to rest for 10 minutes. Knead again for 1 minute and divide the dough into 16-20 even-sized balls. Roll each ball in flour and roll out into a 10-15cm (4-6 inch) circle. Place a frying pan on the heat and when moderately hot place the rolled circle of dough on it; cook for ½-1 minute. Little bubbles will appear; flip over and allow to cook for 1-1½ minutes. Pick the pancake up and check whether little brown specks have appeared on the undersides; if not, then cook for a few seconds more. Use a clean tea towel to press the pancakes gently, this will circulate the steam and cook the pancakes. Prepare the rest of the pancakes in the same way and keep them stacked, wrapped in foil to keep them warm.

To Make Dip
60ml (4 tblsp) sugar
60ml (4 tblsp) bean paste (sweet)
15ml (1 tblsp) sesame oil
15ml (1 tblsp) corn oil or peanut oil
120ml (4 fl oz) water

Other Dips, Ready Prepared
60ml (4 tblsp) Hoi Sin sauce
60ml (4 tblsp) Chinese barbecue sauce

Mix sugar, bean paste and water together. Warm the wok, add the oil and then the sugar mixture. Bring to boil and, when the sugar has melted, remove and put in a bowl. Place the duck on a cutting board and cut thin slices from the breast area and thighs. Place a pancake on an individual plate, cover with a slice of duck and a few strips of onion, spread on a dip of your choice, roll up like a pancake and eat. To make very crisp duck, cut duck into large joints and deep fry them till crispy.

Sweet and Sour Chicken

PREPARATION TIME: 30 minutes
COOKING TIME: 20 minutes

2.5ml (½ tsp) salt
10ml (2 tsp) cornflour or arrowroot
1 chicken breast, cut into 1cm (½") cubes
1 onion, peeled and roughly chopped into 1cm (½") chunks
25g (1oz) bamboo shoots, sliced
1 green pepper, seeded and thinly sliced

2.5cm (1") fresh root ginger, peeled and thinly sliced
2 carrots, scraped and thinly sliced into 2.5cm (1") long pieces
1 garlic clove, peeled and chopped
30ml (2 tblsp) oil

Batter
100g (4oz) plain flour
25g (1oz) cornflour
1 small egg
Oil for deep frying

Sauce
15ml (1 tblsp) soft brown sugar
15ml (1 tblsp) red wine vinegar or white vinegar
15ml (1 tblsp) soya sauce
15ml (1 tblsp) tomato purée
450ml (¾ pint) chicken stock
Pinch monosodium glutamate (optional)
10ml (2 tsp) cornflour or arrowroot

Mix salt and cornflour and roll chicken pieces in it. Make the batter by mixing the sieved flour and cornflour with the egg and sufficient water to make a thick batter. Beat well. Heat oil for deep frying. Dip the chicken pieces into the batter and deep-fry until golden brown and crisp. Drain on absorbent paper and keep warm.

Heat the 30ml (2 tblsp) oil in a wok and stir fry the onions, ginger and garlic for 2-3 minutes. Add the carrots and fry for 2 minutes. Add the green peppers and fry for 2 minutes. Add bamboo shoots, season with salt and stir well. Mix all the sauce ingredients together. Pour over the cooked vegetables. Cook for 2-3 minutes, until the sauce thickens. The sauce should become transparent. Arrange fried chicken pieces on a serving dish and pour the sweet and sour sauce over them. Serve as a side dish.

This page: Peking Duck with Pancakes.

Facing page: Tangerine Peel Chicken (top), Sweet and Sour Chicken (centre left) and Chicken Chow Mein (bottom).

Fish and Seafood

Prawns with Broccoli

PREPARATION TIME: 10 minutes

COOKING TIME: 8-10 minutes

450g (1lb) peeled prawns
Oil for deep frying

Sauce
120ml (4 fl oz) chicken stock
10ml (2 tsp) cornflour
Freshly ground black pepper and salt
 to taste
Pinch monosodium glutamate
 (optional)
5ml (1 tsp) sugar

Seasoning
30ml (2 tblsp) cooked oil, or oil from
 deep frying the prawns
Pinch salt
2.5ml (½ tsp) sugar
Pinch monosodium glutamate
 (optional)
10ml (2 tsp) cornflour

250g (8oz) Chinese broccoli, or
 English broccoli, cut into 8cm (3")
 pieces
1 carrot, peeled and sliced
2 cloves garlic, peeled and chopped
1cm (½") fresh root ginger, peeled
 and chopped

Deep fry the prawns in hot oil for
1-2 minutes. Drain the prawns and
keep on one side. Keep the oil. Mix
the sauce ingredients together. Mix
the seasoning ingredients together
in a separate bowl. Cook the
broccoli in boiling water for 1
minute. Drain and add cold water
to cover. Drain once again and mix
the broccoli with the seasoning
ingredients. Heat the wok and add
30ml (2 tblsp) cooked oil. Add the
carrot, garlic and ginger and stir fry
for 1 minute. Add the broccoli and
stir fry for 1 minute more. Add the
prawns and stir fry for ½ minute
then add the blended sauce
ingredients. Cook gently until the
sauce thickens. Serve immediately.

Shrimps with Beancurd

PREPARATION TIME: 10 minutes

COOKING TIME: 8 minutes

450g (1lb) peeled shrimps

Seasoning
5ml (1 tsp) light soya sauce
Pinch salt
5ml (1 tsp) sugar
5ml (1 tsp) cornflour

2.5cm (1") fresh root ginger, peeled
 and finely chopped
30ml (2 tblsp) oil
1 clove of garlic, peeled and chopped
1 red chilli, chopped
2-3 beancurd cakes, cubed
60ml (4 tblsp) chicken stock
5ml (1 tsp) cornflour
30ml (2 tblsp) water

Mix the shrimps with the
seasoning ingredients and half of
the ginger. Heat the oil and stir fry
the ginger and shrimps for 2
minutes. Add the garlic and fry for
1 minute. Add the chilli, cubed
beancurd and stock. Simmer for 2-
3 minutes. Mix the cornflour with
the water and remaining crushed
ginger and pour over the shrimp
mixture. Simmer gently until the
sauce thickens. Serve immediately.

Prawns in Hot Sauce

PREPARATION TIME: 10 minutes

COOKING TIME: 6 minutes

350g (12oz) cooked unshelled
 prawns

Seasoning
5ml (1 tsp) malt vinegar
5ml (1 tsp) Shao Hsing wine
Pinch salt

Sauce
5ml (1 tsp) cornflour mixed with
 15ml (1 tblsp) water
10ml (2 tsp) tomato purée
Salt and freshly ground black pepper
 to taste
10ml (2 tsp) sugar

2.5ml (½ tsp) monosodium
 glutamate (optional)
5ml (1 tsp) hot chilli sauce
180ml (6 fl oz) chicken stock
30ml (2 tblsp) cooked oil

Wash prawns and drain well. Mix
the seasoning ingredients together.
Mix the sauce ingredients together
in a separate bowl. Heat the oil in a
wok and deep fry the prawns for 1
minute. Remove the prawns and
drain. Keep the oil. Reheat the wok
and add 10ml (2 tsp) oil and stir fry
the onion, celery and garlic for 1
minute. Add prawns and the
blended sauce ingredients. Bring to
the boil and simmer gently for 3-4
minutes. Stir in the seasoning
mixture.

Fish in Wine Sauce

PREPARATION TIME: 20 minutes

COOKING TIME: 15 minutes

Marinade
1.25ml (¼ tsp) salt
1 egg white
10ml (2 tsp) cornflour
5ml (1 tsp) wine vinegar

275-350g (10-12oz) mullet or carp
 fillet, cut into 5cm (2 inch) slices
Oil for deep frying
250ml (8 fl oz) chicken stock

Prawns in Hot Sauce (top right), Shrimps with Bean Curd (centre right) and Prawns with Broccoli (bottom right).

Seasoning

Pinch monosodium glutamate
  (optional)
Pinch salt
Pinch freshly ground black pepper
5ml (1 tsp) sugar
10ml (2 tsp) cornflour
15ml (1 tblsp) water
1 cloud ear fungus, soaked and
  boiled for 2 minutes, and then
  chopped
2 dried Chinese mushrooms, soaked
  and sliced

Mix the marinade ingredients
together. Marinate the fish in the
marinade for 10 minutes. Heat a
generous quantity of oil in the wok

and deep fry the fish pieces, a few
at a time, until the flesh is white.
Remove and drain the fish. Keep
the oil for future use. Clean the
wok. Add the chicken stock to the
wok and bring to the boil. Simmer
gently and stir in the seasoning
ingredients. Simmer for a few
seconds and then add the
cornflour blended with the water.
Add the fish and simmer until the
sauce thickens. Add the fungus
and mushrooms. Simmer for 1
minute. Serve immediately.

Fish with Chicken and Vegetables

PREPARATION TIME: 25 minutes

COOKING TIME: 15 minutes

450g (1lb) pomfret, plaice or lemon
  sole fillets, cut into 5cm (2 inch)
  pieces
225g (8oz) boned chicken, cut into
  5cm (2 inch) slices
6 dried Chinese mushrooms, soaked
  and sliced
50g (2oz) button mushrooms, sliced
50g (2oz) bamboo shoots, sliced
50g (2oz) mustard green, kale, or
  broccoli or 4 asparagus tips
100g (4oz) mixed vegetables (peas,
  carrots, bean sprouts, etc)
1 small onion, peeled and sliced
5ml (1 tsp) salt
Cooked oil

Marinade

1.25ml (¼ tsp) salt
5ml (1 tsp) white pepper
2.5ml (½ tsp) monosodium
  glutamate (optional)
10ml (2 tsp) cornflour
15ml (1 tblsp) cooked oil
1.25ml (¼ tsp) sesame oil

Sauce

250ml (8 fl oz) chicken stock
Salt to taste
Freshly ground black pepper to taste
2.5ml (½ tsp) monosodium
  glutamate (optional)
10ml (2 tsp) cooked oil
5ml (1 tsp) lemon juice

Wash the fish and drain. Mix the
marinade ingredients together and
marinate fish for 10-15 minutes.
Blanch the mustard green, kale or
broccoli in boiling, salted water for
1 minute. Drain and keep on one
side. Heat the wok with 15ml (1
tblsp) cooked oil and stir fry the
mixed vegetables and the onions
for 2 minutes. Add the mustard
green and stir fry for 1 minute.
Drain and remove onto a plate.
Brush a deep plate with cooked oil
and arrange the drained fish,
mushrooms, chicken and bamboo
shoots in alternate rows. Place the
dish over a steamer. Cover and
steam over boiling water for 7
minutes until cooked. Remove the
steamer from heat and keep on one
side. Heat the wok and add the
sauce ingredients and fish
marinade. Bring to the boil and
simmer for 1 minute, until
thickened. Put the steamed fish,
mushrooms etc. onto a serving
plate and pour the hot sauce over
the top. Serve immediately.

Fish with Vegetables and Bean Curd

PREPARATION TIME: 20 minutes

COOKING TIME: 15 minutes

4 squares bean curd, cut into 2.5cm
  (1 inch) squares

Sauce B

15ml (1 tblsp) Shao Hsing wine
15ml (1 tblsp) dark soya sauce
15ml (1 tblsp) light soya sauce
10ml (2 tsp) sugar
Pinch salt
Pinch white pepper
900ml (1½ pints) chicken stock
225g (8oz) cod fillet, cut into 5cm (2
  inch) slices

Seasoning for Fish A

2.5ml (½ tsp) salt
2.5ml (½ tsp) Shao Hsing wine
22.5ml (1½ tblsp) cornflour
45ml (3 tblsp) oil

Seasoning for Cabbage C

2.5ml (½ tsp) sugar
Pinch salt
5ml (1 tsp) cornflour
2.5cm (1 inch) fresh root ginger,
  peeled and shredded
2 spring onions, chopped

22.5ml (1½ tblsp) cornflour mixed
  with 30ml (2 tblsp) water
25g (1oz) bean sprouts
Few slices of pepper, diced
1 small carrot, chopped
25g (1oz) shelled or frozen peas

Soak the bean curd in cold water
for 2 minutes. Drain well. Mix the
sauce B ingredients and keep on
one side. Wash the fish and drain
well. Mix seasoning A ingredients
and marinate fish for 10-12
minutes. Heat the wok and add
half the oil. When very hot, add
the cabbage and seasoning C
ingredients and stir fry for about 2
minutes. Drain the cabbage well.
Discard any liquid. Heat wok and
add the remaining oil. Add the
ginger and onions and stir fry for 1
minute. Add sauce B ingredients
and bring to the boil. Add fish and
boil for 1 minute. Add the
beancurd and simmer over a low
heat for 5-6 minutes. (The
bean curd should become spongy
to the touch.) Add the blended
cornflour and water. Stir and
simmer until the sauce thickens.
Add the cabbage and simmer for a
further 2 minutes. Serve
immediately.

Boiled Prawns

PREPARATION TIME: 5 minutes,
plus 10 minutes for the sauce

COOKING TIME: 10-15 minutes

Sauce

30ml (2 tblsp) dark soya sauce
45ml (3 tblsp) light soya sauce
1cm (½") fresh root ginger, peeled
  and shredded
2 spring onions, finely chopped
1 red chilli, seeded and shredded
60ml (4 tblsp) cooked oil
10ml (2 tsp) tomato purée

1kg (2 lb) medium or large
  uncooked prawns in their shells
Salt

Mix the sauce ingredients together.
Wash the prawns and drain. Place
the prawns into a wire basket and
lower into a large pan of boiling,
salted water. Boil for 10-12
minutes. Drain. Serve the drained
hot prawns with small bowls of
sauce for dipping.

Cantonese Prawns

PREPARATION TIME: 10 minutes

COOKING TIME: 15 minutes

45ml (3 tblsp) oil
2 cloves garlic, finely crushed
450g (1lb) peeled prawns
5cm (2") root ginger, peeled and
  finely chopped
100g (4oz) uncooked pork or bacon,
  finely chopped

Sauce

15ml (1 tblsp) rice wine or dry sherry
15ml (1 tblsp) light soya sauce
5ml (1 tsp) sugar
250ml (8 fl oz) stock or water
15ml (1 tblsp) cornflour mixed with
  30ml (2 tblsp) stock or water

2-3 spring onions, chopped
2 eggs, lightly beaten

Heat 15ml (1 tblsp) oil in a wok.
Add the garlic and fry for 1 minute.
Add the prawns and stir fry for 4-5
minutes. Remove to a dish. Keep
warm. Add the remaining oil to the
wok and fry the ginger and pork for
3-4 minutes until it loses its
colour. Add the mixed sauce
ingredients to the wok and cook
for 1 minute. Add the onions and
cook for 1 minute. Add the beaten
eggs and cook for 1-2 minutes,
without stirring, until it sets. Spoon
the egg mixture over the prawns.

Alternatively, add the prawns along with the beaten eggs. Allow the eggs to set and then mix gently. Serve at once.

Prawns and Ginger

PREPARATION TIME: 10 minutes

COOKING TIME: 10 minutes

30ml (2 tblsp) oil
675g (1½ lb) peeled prawns
2.5cm (1") fresh root ginger, peeled and finely chopped
2 cloves garlic, peeled and finely chopped
2-3 spring onions, chopped lengthways into 2.5cm (1") pieces
1 leek, white part only, cut into strips.
100g (4oz) shelled peas
175g (6oz) bean sprouts

Seasoning
30ml (2 tblsp) dark soya sauce
5ml (1 tsp) sugar
Pinch monosodium glutamate (optional)
Pinch of salt

Heat the oil in a wok and stir fry the prawns for 2-3 minutes. Remove the prawns to a dish. Reheat the oil and add the ginger and garlic and fry for 1 minute. Add the onions and stir fry for 1 minute. Add the leek, peas and bean sprouts. Stir fry for 2-3 minutes. Sprinkle over the seasoning ingredients and return the prawns to the wok. Cover and cook for 2 minutes. Serve immediately.

Shrimp and Cauliflower

PREPARATION TIME: 15 minutes

COOKING TIME: 14-15 minutes

45ml (3 tblsp) oil
1 clove of garlic, peeled and finely chopped
450g (1lb) shrimps, peeled
275g (10oz) cauliflower florets, cut into smaller pieces
250ml (8 fl oz) water or stock
Salt to taste
175g (6oz) shelled peas

Facing page: Fish with Vegetables and Bean Curd (top), Fish in Wine Sauce (centre right), Fish with Chicken and Vegetables (bottom). This page: Prawns and Ginger (top), Boiled Prawns (centre) and Cantonese Prawns (bottom right).

Sauce

10ml (2 tsp) cornflour
30ml (2 tblsp) stock or water
Freshly ground black pepper to taste

Heat the oil in a wok and fry the
garlic for 2 minutes. Add the
shrimps and cook for 3 minutes.
Remove the shrimps. Add
cauliflower and fry for 2-3 minutes,
stirring constantly. Add stock,
cover and simmer for five minutes.
Add salt to taste and the peas and
cook for a further 2-3 minutes.
Return the shrimps to the wok and
stir well. Add the blended sauce
ingredients and gently simmer until
it thickens. Serve immediately.

Snow Peas with Shrimps

PREPARATION TIME: 10 minutes

COOKING TIME: 6-8 minutes

5ml (1 tsp) cornflour
5ml (1 tsp) sugar
5ml (1 tsp) dark soya sauce
15ml (1 tblsp) water
45ml (3 tblsp) oil
450g (1lb) peeled shrimps
180ml (6 fl oz) chicken stock
2.5ml (½ tsp) salt
100g (4oz) snow peas (mange tout)
75g (3oz) water chestnuts, sliced
1 small onion, peeled and cut into
small pieces
1 stem celery, cut into 5mm (¼")
pieces
Pinch monosodium glutamate
(optional)

Mix together the cornflour, sugar,
soya sauce and water. Heat the oil
in a wok. Add the shrimps and stir
fry for 2 minutes. Add the stock,
salt, snow peas, water chestnuts,
onions and celery. Cover and cook
for 2 minutes. Stir in the
monosodium glutamate. Stir in the
cornflour mixture and simmer
gently until the sauce thickens.
Serve as a side dish.

Prawns with Cashew Nuts

PREPARATION TIME: 10 minutes

COOKING TIME: 7-8 minutes

45ml (3 tblsp) oil
50-75g (2-3oz) cashew nuts
10ml (2 tsp) cornflour
250ml (8 fl oz) chicken stock or
water

1 onion, peeled and cut into small
pieces
25g (1oz) sliced green beans
50g (2oz) Chinese cabbage or white
cabbage, shredded
50g (2oz) bamboo shoots, sliced
450g (1lb) peeled prawns
Salt and freshly ground black pepper
to taste
4 rings pineapple, cut into chunks
Pinch monosodium glutamate
(optional)

Heat 15ml (1 tblsp) oil in a wok
and stir fry the cashew nuts until
light brown. Remove the nuts and
keep on one side. Mix the
cornflour with 30ml (2 tblsp) water
or stock and keep on one side.
Reheat the wok with the remaining
oil and fry the onion for 1 minute.
Add the beans, cabbage and
bamboo shoots and stir fry for 2-3
minutes. Add the cashew nuts and
prawns and then add the remaining
stock, salt and pepper, and the
pineapple. Simmer for 1 minute
and then add the MSG and

cornflour mixture and cook until
the sauce thickens. Serve
immediately.

**Shrimp and Cauliflower (top
right), Prawns with Cashew
Nuts (centre left) and Snow
Peas with Shrimps (bottom).**

Vegetables

Braised Cauliflower with Chilli

PREPARATION TIME: 5 minutes

COOKING TIME: 10 minutes

60ml (4 tblsp) oil
2.5cm (1 inch) fresh root ginger,
    peeled and thinly sliced
1 small cauliflower, cut into 2.5cm (1
    inch) florets
2-3 green or red chillis, sliced into
    quarters and seeded
3 spring onions
Salt to taste
5ml (1 tsp) sugar
300ml (½ pint) chicken stock
5ml (1 tsp) cornflour or arrowroot
15ml (1 tblsp) water

Heat the wok and add the oil. Stir
fry the ginger for 1 minute. Reduce
the heat and add the cauliflower
and chillis. Stir fry for 3-4 minutes.
Add the spring onions, season with
salt and sprinkle with sugar. Mix
for 1 minute and then add the
stock. Cover and cook for 2
minutes. Add the blended
cornflour and water and stir over
the heat until the sauce has
thickened.

Fried Bean Curd with Mushrooms

PREPARATION TIME: 15 minutes

COOKING TIME: 12-15 minutes

225g (8oz) mushrooms (button or
    open) sliced

Seasoning
15ml (1 tblsp) rice wine or dry sherry
10ml (2 tsp) sugar
4 dried Chinese mushrooms, soaked
    and sliced
Pinch bicarbonate of soda
225g (8oz) mustard green or spinach,
    cut into 7.5cm (3 inch) pieces
4 squares bean curd (tau fu), cubed
Oil
2.5cm (1 inch) fresh root ginger,
    peeled and shredded
2 spring onions, chopped
50g (2oz) cooked ham, shredded

Sauce
15ml (1 tblsp) oyster sauce
5ml (1 tsp) dark soya sauce

15ml (1 tblsp) cornflour
60ml (4 tblsp) stock or water
Freshly ground black pepper

Blanch the fresh mushrooms in
water for 1 minute. Drain the
mushrooms and discard the water.
Mix the seasoning ingredients
together and marinate the
mushrooms for 5-6 minutes.
Discard marinade. Bring 1.2 litres
(2 pints) of water to the boil and
add the bicarbonate of soda and
salt. Blanch the greens for 2
minutes. Drain the greens. Discard
water. Sprinkle 2.5ml (½ tsp) salt
over the bean curd. Deep fry in hot
oil until golden brown. Drain and
remove. Heat 30ml (2 tblsp) oil in
the wok and stir fry the ginger,
onions and ham for 2-3 minutes.
Return the mushrooms to the wok
and mix with the ginger and
onions. Add the blended sauce
ingredients and bring to boil. Add
the bean curd and simmer until the
sauce thickens. Arrange the greens
on a dish and pour the sauce over
them. Sprinkle with freshly ground
black pepper.

Fried Vegetables with Ginger

PREPARATION TIME: 10 minutes

COOKING TIME: 13-15 minutes

1kg (2¼ lb) mixed Chinese green
    vegetables (cabbage, spinach, kale,
    broccoli, Chinese leaf etc.)
50g (2oz) snow peas (mange tout)
5ml (1 tsp) bicarbonate of soda
10ml (2 tsp) sugar
5ml (1 tsp) salt
15ml (1 tblsp) cooked oil
45ml (3 tblsp) oil
2.5cm (1 inch) fresh root ginger,
    peeled and shredded
1 green pepper, seeded and diced
1 green or red chilli, sliced into strips

Sauce
10ml (2 tsp) dark soya sauce
5ml (1 tsp) sugar
250ml (8 fl oz) chicken stock
10ml (2 tsp) cornflour
5ml (1 tsp) five spice powder

To Serve
2.5ml (½ tsp) sesame oil
Freshly ground black pepper to taste

Cut greens into 7.5cm (3 inch)
pieces. Bring a large pan of water to
the boil and add the seasoning
ingredients. Add the snow peas
and greens and cook for 4-5
minutes. Drain green vegetables
and discard water. Add 15ml (1
tblsp) oil to the vegetables and
keep covered. Heat the remaining
oil in the wok and stir fry the ginger
for 1 minute. Add the green
pepper and chillis and stir fry for 1-
2 minutes. Add the blended sauce
ingredients and stir well. Simmer
gently for 3-4 minutes. Add the
green vegetables and cook for 1
minute. Serve immediately,
sprinkled with sesame oil and
pepper.

Bamboo Shoots with Green Vegetables

PREPARATION TIME: 10 minutes

COOKING TIME: 10-12 minutes

Oil for cooking
225g (8oz) spinach, or chopped
    broccoli

Seasoning
120ml (4 fl oz) chicken stock or water
1.25ml (¼ tsp) monosodium
    glutamate (optional)
1.25ml (¼ tsp) salt
1.25ml (¼ tsp) sugar
100g (4oz) bamboo shoots, sliced

Sauce
5ml (1 tsp) light soya sauce
Pinch monosodium glutamate
5ml (1 tsp) cornflour
10ml (2 tsp) water
15ml (1 tblsp) cooked oil

Heat 30ml (2 tblsp) oil in the wok.
Fry the spinach for 2 minutes and
add the mixed seasoning
ingredients. Simmer for 1 minute
and remove from the wok onto a

**Fried Vegetables with Ginger
(top right), Mustard Green with
Crab Sauce (centre left) and
Fried Bean Curd with
Mushrooms (bottom).**

peeled and sliced
2-3 spring onions, chopped
225-275g (8-10oz) chicken,
shredded (cooked or uncooked)

Seasoning
30ml (2 tblsp) light soya sauce
2.5ml (½ tsp) sugar
15ml (1 tblsp) cornflour or arrowroot
30ml (2 tblsp) stock or water, if
needed

Heat 60ml (4 tblsp) oil in the wok and stir fry the garlic for 2 minutes. Add the aubergine, which will soak up all the oil. Stir fry for 3-4 minutes, stirring constantly to avoid burning. Add the bean paste, chilli powder and salt to taste, and mix well. Add the chicken stock. Cover and cook for 4-6 minutes, simmering gently. Remove the aubergine and arrange on a dish. Save the sauce. Clean the wok and heat the remaining oil. Stir fry the ginger for 1 minute. Add the onions and chicken and stir fry for 2 minutes. Add the blended seasoning ingredients and the reserved aubergine sauce and simmer gently until it thickens. Pour over the aubergine and serve immediately.

Szechuan Aubergine

PREPARATION TIME: 15 minutes

COOKING TIME: 18-20 minutes

Oil
1 large European aubergine or
450g (1lb) oriental aubergines, cut
into 5cm (2 inch) long and 1cm
(½ inch) thick strips
3 cloves garlic, peeled and finely
sliced
2.5cm (1 inch) fresh root ginger,
peeled and shredded
1 onion, peeled and finely chopped
2 spring onions, chopped
100g (4oz) cooked and shredded
chicken
1 red or green chilli, cut into strips

Seasoning
120ml (4 fl oz) chicken stock
5ml (1 tsp) sugar
5ml (1 tsp) red vinegar or wine
vinegar
2.5ml (½ tsp) salt
2.5ml (½ tsp) freshly ground black
pepper

Sauce
5ml (1 tsp) cornflour
15ml (1 tblsp) water
5ml (1 tsp) sesame oil

dish. Heat the wok and add 15ml (1 tblsp) oil. Add the bamboo shoots and fry for 1-2 minutes. Return the spinach mixture to the wok. Cook for 3 minutes. Mix together the ingredients for thickening the sauce. Add to the wok and cook for 1-2 minutes. Serve with roast Peking duck, or as a side dish.

Braised Aubergine and Chicken with Chilli

PREPARATION TIME: 10 minutes

COOKING TIME: about 15 minutes

90ml (3 fl oz) oil
2 cloves of garlic, peeled and sliced

450g (1lb) aubergine, cut into 5x6cm
(2x2½ inch) pieces
15ml (1 tblsp) soya bean paste (or
canned red kidney beans, made
into paste)
2.5ml (½ tsp) ground dry chilli or
chilli powder
Salt
450ml (¾ pint) chicken stock
2.5cm (1 inch) fresh root ginger,

Heat the wok and add 45ml (3 tblsp) oil. Add the aubergine and stir fry for 4-5 minutes. The aubergines absorb a lot of oil; keep stirring or else they will burn. Remove from wok and keep on one side. Heat the wok and add 30ml (2 tblsp) oil. Add the garlic and ginger and fry for 1 minute. Add the onions and fry for 2 minutes. Add the chicken and chilli. Cook for 1 minute. Return the aubergines to the wok. Add the blended seasoning ingredients and simmer for 6-7 minutes. Stir in the blended sauce ingredients and simmer until the sauce thickens. Serve with extra sesame oil if desired. This dish goes well with Yung Chow fried rice or rice supreme.

Lettuce and Bean Sprouts with Soya Sauce

PREPARATION TIME: 15 minutes

COOKING TIME: 5 minutes

100g (4oz) bean sprouts (moong or soya)
225g (8oz) sweet lettuce
15ml (1 tblsp) oil
2.5cm (1 inch) fresh root ginger, peeled and shredded
1 green or red chilli, seeded and split in half
Salt and freshly ground black pepper

Sauce
30ml (2 tblsp) light soya sauce
5ml (1 tsp) dark soya sauce
10ml (2 tsp) medium white wine or rice wine
2.5ml (½ tsp) sugar
Salt and freshly ground black pepper to taste
2.5ml (½ tsp) sesame oil

Trim the bean sprouts by pinching off the grey and brown ends, as they impart a bitter taste to the dish. Pick off bean seed skin if using soya beans. Cut soya bean sprouts in 2-3 pieces. Rinse in cold water and drain. Wash and drain lettuce before shredding into 5cm (2 inch) pieces. Heat the oil in the wok and stir fry the ginger and chilli for 1 minute. Add the lettuce and toss

for 1 minute. Drain and remove on to a plate. Place the bean sprouts in a colander and pour boiling water over them. Drain thoroughly and add to the lettuce. Sprinkle with salt and pepper and keep covered. Mix the sauce ingredients together in the wok. Stir over the heat until blended. Pour this sauce over the vegetables and serve immediately.

Sweet and Sour Cabbage

PREPARATION TIME: 10 minutes

COOKING TIME: 10 minutes

450g (1lb) white cabbage, shredded
2.5ml (½ tsp) bicarbonate of soda
5ml (1 tsp) salt
10ml (2 tsp) sugar
15ml (1 tblsp) oil

Sauce
30ml (2 tblsp) sugar
30ml (2 tblsp) wine vinegar
250ml (8 fl oz) chicken stock or water
Pinch salt

15ml (1 tblsp) cornflour or arrowroot
Few drops red food colouring
5ml (1 tsp) tomato purée

Boil the cabbage in a large pan of water with the bicarbonate of soda, salt and sugar for 2-3 minutes. Drain the cabbage and discard the boiling water. Keep the cabbage in cold water for 5 minutes. Drain and keep on one side. Heat the wok and add the oil. Fry the cabbage until it is heated through. Remove on to a serving dish. Add the well-stirred sauce ingredients to the wok and gently bring to the boil, stirring. Stir over the heat until the sauce thickens. Pour over the cabbage and serve immediately.

Facing page: Bamboo Shoots with Green Vegetables (top right), Sweet and Sour Cabbage (centre left), Szechuan Aubergine (bottom).

This page: Lettuce and Bean Sprouts with Soya Sauce (left), Braised Aubergine and Chicken with Chilli (centre) and Braised Cauliflower with Chilli (right).

Egg Dishes and Curry

Lamb Curry

PREPARATION TIME: 15 minutes

COOKING TIME: 50 minutes

30ml (2 tblsp) oil
1 onion, peeled and chopped
2.5cm (1 inch) fresh root ginger, peeled and chopped
2 cloves of garlic, chopped
450g (1lb) lean, boned lamb, cut into cubes
1-2 carrots, scraped and sliced
5ml (1 tsp) five spice mixture
Salt to taste
2 chillis, chopped
15ml (1 tblsp) tomato purée
10ml (2 tblsp) cornflour
1 green pepper, seeded and chopped

Heat the oil and fry the onion for 2 minutes. Add the ginger and garlic and fry for 1 minute. Add the lamb and carrots and stir fry for 3-4 minutes. Sprinkle over the five spice powder and add the salt, chillis and tomato purée. Stir in 300ml (½ pint) water. Cover and simmer for 30-35 minutes. Mix 30ml (2 tblsp) water with the cornflour and add to the curry. Add the green pepper and simmer for 5 minutes. Serve with rice.

Prawn Curry

PREPARATION TIME: 10 minutes

COOKING TIME: 8 minutes

30ml (2 tblsp) oil
1 onion, peeled and chopped
1 carrot, cut into strips
75g (3oz) snow peas (mange tout)
2.5cm (1 inch) fresh root ginger, peeled and chopped
2 cloves garlic, chopped
450g (1lb) prawns, peeled
7.5ml (1½ tsp) curry powder
Salt to taste
2 green chillis, sliced
10ml (2 tblsp) cornflour

Heat the oil and fry the onions for 2 minutes. Add the carrot and snow peas and fry for 2 minutes. Add the ginger, garlic and prawns and stir fry for 1-2 minutes. Sprinkle over the curry powder and add the salt, green chillis and 300ml (½ pint) water. Mix the cornflour with 15ml (1 tblsp) water and add to the curry. Cook gently until the curry thickens. Serve with rice.

Chicken Curry

PREPARATION TIME: 15 minutes

COOKING TIME: 40 minutes

30ml (2 tblsp) oil
1 onion, peeled and chopped
2 cloves of garlic, peeled and chopped
2.5cm (1 inch) fresh root ginger, peeled and finely chopped
1.5kg (3lb) chicken, boned and cut into small pieces
10ml (2 tsp) curry powder
5ml (1 tsp) chilli powder
2.5ml (½ tsp) salt
100g (4oz) mixed frozen vegetables
1 green pepper, seeded and chopped
10ml (2 tsp) cornflour

Heat the oil and fry the onions for 2 minutes. Add the garlic, ginger and chicken and fry gently for 5 minutes. Add the curry powder, chilli powder, salt and 450ml (¾ pint) of water. Cover and cook gently until the chicken is tender. Add the mixed vegetables and green pepper and cook for 3-4 minutes. Add the cornflour, dissolved in 30ml (2 tblsp) water, and simmer until the sauce thickens. Serve with plain boiled rice.

Shrimp Fu Yung

PREPARATION TIME: 10 minutes

COOKING TIME: 4 minutes for filling; 3-4 minutes for each pancake

Oil
1-2 cloves of garlic, chopped
100g (4oz) shrimps, peeled
100g (4oz) green beans, sliced
1 carrot, shredded
6 eggs
Salt and freshly ground black pepper to taste
250ml (8 fl oz) chicken stock
1.25ml (¼ tsp) salt
10ml (2 tsp) soya sauce
5ml (1 tsp) sugar
5ml (1 tsp) vinegar
5ml (1 tsp) cornflour

Heat 30ml (2 tblsp) oil in a wok. Add the garlic and stir fry for 1 minute. Add the shrimps and stir fry for 1 minute. Add the beans and carrots and stir fry for 2 minutes. Remove and keep on one side. Beat the eggs with salt and pepper to taste, and add the cooled shrimp mixture. Clean the wok and heat 5ml (1 tsp) oil. Pour in 60ml (4 tblsp) of the egg mixture and cook like a pancake. When the egg is set, turn the pancake over and cook on the other side until lightly golden. Place on a warm platter and keep warm.

To Make the Sauce
Beat the stock with the other sauce ingredients and stir over a gentle heat until the sauce thickens. Serve the pancakes with this sauce. Makes 6-8 servings.

Egg Fu Yung

PREPARATION TIME: 5 minutes

COOKING TIME: 8-10 minutes

6 eggs
22.5ml (1½ tblsp) soya sauce
3-4 spring onions, chopped
Salt and freshly ground black pepper to taste
45ml (3 tblsp) oil
100g (4oz) bean sprouts

Beat the eggs and soya sauce together and add the spring onions and salt and pepper to taste. Heat the oil in a frying pan or wok and stir fry the bean sprouts for 2-3 minutes. Pour in the beaten egg mixture. Leave over a moderate heat to set and then put under the grill to set and brown the top. Cut into wedges and serve immediately. Alternatively, stir the mixture while it is cooking so that it turns out like scrambled egg.

Prawns in Egg Custard

PREPARATION TIME: 5 minutes

COOKING TIME: 20 minutes

8 eggs
Salt and freshly ground black pepper to taste
Pinch monosodium glutamate (optional)
5ml (1 tsp) Shao Hsing wine
300ml (½ pint) chicken stock
300ml (½ pint) water
450g (1lb) prawns, peeled
10ml (2 tsp) cooked oil

Beat the eggs in a bowl, add the seasoning, MSG and wine. Bring the stock and water to the boil and add to the eggs. Add prawns and set the bowl over a steamer. Cover and steam over simmering water for about 15-20 minutes, until the custard has set. Serve with the cooked oil spooned over the top.

Stir Fried Eggs with Shredded Meats and Vegetables

PREPARATION TIME: 15-20 minutes

COOKING TIME: 15 minutes

50g (2oz) cooked chicken, shredded
75g (3oz) cooked pork or beef, shredded
Salt to taste
1.25ml (¼ tsp) soya sauce
60ml (4 tblsp) oil
4 eggs, beaten
2 spring onions, chopped
50g (2oz) dried mushrooms, soaked and sliced
50g (2oz) button mushrooms, sliced
2 cloud ear fungus, boiled in water for 3 minutes and thinly sliced
175g (6oz) Chinese white cabbage, broccoli or green leafy cabbage, shredded.
1-2 green or red chillis, chopped
2 sprigs Chinese parsley, chopped
Pinch monosodium glutamate (optional)

Put the chicken and pork into a bowl with 1.25ml (¼ tsp) salt and the soya sauce. Leave for 10 minutes. Heat the wok and add 30ml (2 tblsp) oil. Add the beaten eggs and stir fry for 2-3 minutes until they resemble scrambled egg. Keep on one side. Reheat the wok and add the remaining oil. Fry the onions and meats for 2 minutes. Remove from the wok and keep on one side. Stir fry the cabbage and chillis in the wok for 1-2 minutes. Cover and gently cook in its own juice until tender – approx 3-4 minutes. Return the meats, mushrooms and egg to the cabbage and add the parsley and MSG. Stir fry for 1-2 minutes. Serve with extra soya sauce and Shao Hsing wine sprinkled over it, if desired.

Lamb Curry (right), Prawn Curry (below) and Chicken Curry (bottom).

Marbled Eggs

PREPARATION TIME: 10 minutes

COOKING TIME: 1 hour 10 minutes to 1 hour 15 minutes

These are eaten cold, dipped in a sauce, as a starter or a snack. Allow 1 egg per person.

6-8 eggs
45ml (3 tblsp) tea leaves
2.5cm (1 inch) cinnamon stick
2-3 star anise
30ml (2 tblsp) dark soya sauce
30ml (2 tblsp) light soya sauce

Boil the eggs for 8-10 minutes until hard boiled. Drain and cool quickly by placing in iced water. Tap each egg shell with the back of a spoon until cracks appear all over. Bring enough water to the boil to cover the eggs. Add tea leaves, cinnamon, star anise, soya sauces and stir. Add the eggs and simmer gently for at least 1 hour. Allow to cool and then shell before serving.

Egg Pancakes with Filling

PREPARATION TIME: 10 minutes

COOKING TIME: 6-7 minutes for each pancake

6 eggs
Salt and freshly ground black pepper
    to taste
100g (4oz) lean pork, finely chopped
    or ground
50g (2oz) button mushrooms,
    chopped
5ml (1 tsp) rice wine or dry sherry
5ml (1 tsp) light soya sauce
2.5ml (½ tsp) sugar
2.5ml (½ tsp) fresh root ginger, minced
Oil

Beat the eggs and season with salt and pepper. Mix the pork with the mushrooms, wine, soya sauce, sugar and ginger. Add salt and pepper to taste and mix well. Heat the wok and add 5ml (1 tsp) oil. Spoon in 30ml (2 tblsp) of the beaten egg and spread into a 7½cm (3 inch) circle. Place 10ml (2 tsp) filling into the centre of the egg. When the underside of the egg sets but the top is still moist, fold the egg circle over to make a crescent shape; press gently to seal the edges. Cook for 4 minutes on a low heat to cook the filling. Make the remaining pancakes in the same way. Serve with a chilli sauce or dip, or with stir fried vegetables as a main dish.

Noodles with Pork Fu Yung

PREPARATION TIME: 20 minutes

COOKING TIME: about 20 minutes

2.5ml (½ tsp) bicarbonate of soda
15ml (1 tblsp) water
225g (8oz) pork, thinly sliced
225g (8oz) cake noodles
10ml (2 tsp) cornflour
Few drops sesame oil
Salt and freshly ground black pepper
    to taste

2.5ml (½ tsp) sugar
Oil
2 cloves of garlic, finely chopped
2.5cm (1 inch) fresh root ginger,
    peeled and sliced
2-3 spring onions, chopped
6 eggs, well beaten

Mix the bicarbonate of soda and the water together. Mix in the pork and marinate for 10-12 minutes. Drain. Cook the noodles in boiling, salted water for 3-4 minutes. Drain, rinse in cold water and drain once again. Toss in 15ml (1 tblsp) oil. Heat 30ml (2 tblsp) oil in the wok

and brown the garlic. Add 5ml (1 tsp) salt and the noodles and stir fry for 3-4 minutes, until they turn light brown. Remove and keep on one side. Heat sufficient oil for deep frying in the wok and deep fry the pork for 3-4 minutes, drain and remove. Tip off the oil. Heat 15ml (1 tblsp) oil in the wok. Add the ginger and onions and stir fry for 1-2 minutes. Add the pork and then pour in the beaten eggs, mixing well. Add the cornflour, sesame oil and sugar and cook until the mixture thickens. Pour over the noodles and serve immediately.

This page: Marbled Eggs (top), Noodles with Pork Fu Yung (centre right) and Stir Fried Eggs with Shredded Meats and Vegetables (bottom left).

Facing page: Prawns in Egg Custard (top left), Egg Pancakes with Filling (top right), Shrimp Fu Yung (centre left) and Egg Fu Yung (bottom right).

Rice and Noodles

Rice with Minced Beef

PREPARATION TIME: 10 minutes

COOKING TIME: 25 minutes

30ml (2 tblsp) cooking oil
225g (8oz) minced beef
3 spring onions, chopped
1.25cm (½ inch) fresh root ginger,
   peeled and sliced
2 cloves garlic, peeled and sliced
15ml (1 tblsp) soya sauce
1 green pepper, seeded and chopped
450g (1lb) rice, thoroughly washed
2.5ml (½ tsp) salt
5ml (1 tsp) freshly ground black
   pepper, or to taste

Heat the oil and fry the mince,
onions, ginger and garlic for 5
minutes. Add the soya sauce and
green pepper and fry for 5-6
minutes. Cook the rice with 2.5cm
(1 inch) water above the rice level
with the salt for 5-6 minutes or
until the rice is semi-cooked and
the water is almost absorbed.
Spread the mince evenly over the
rice. Cover and cook for 6-8
minutes over a very gentle heat.
Remove and serve well mixed.
Season with salt and pepper to
taste.

Assorted Meat Congee

PREPARATION TIME: 20 minutes

COOKING TIME: 1 hour
                           45 minutes

450g (1lb) rice
Scant 2½ litres (4 pints) chicken
   stock
100g (4oz) tripe, well washed and
   chopped (optional)
100g (4oz) pig's or lamb's liver, sliced
100g (4oz) cooked beef, ham, lamb,
   chicken or pork, chopped
100g (4oz) white fish fillets, thinly
   sliced
5ml (1 tsp) sesame oil
3 spring onions, chopped
7.5ml (1½ tsp) salt, or to taste
7.5ml (1½ tsp) freshly ground black
   pepper
1.25cm (½ inch) fresh root ginger,
   peeled and sliced

Wash the rice well and put it into a
large saucepan. Add the chicken

stock and the tripe (if used). Cook
gently for 1-1½ hours or until the
tripe is well cooked and the rice has
become a soft pulp. In a separate
saucepan, boil the sliced liver for 5
minutes in water. Drain and add to
the rice. Add the cooked meat,
fish, sesame oil, half the onions, salt
and pepper and the slices of ginger.
Cook for further 10-15 minutes
covered. Pour into large bowls and
serve topped with the remaining
chopped onions.

Rice Supreme

PREPARATION TIME: 10 minutes

COOKING TIME: 15 minutes

45ml (3 tblsp) cooking oil
15ml (1 tblsp) light soya sauce
2 eggs, beaten
1 small onion, peeled and finely
   sliced
50g (2oz) shrimps, peeled
50g (2oz) prawns, peeled

50g (2oz) white fish, cubed
2 spring onions, finely chopped
50g (2oz) green pepper, seeded and
   cut into strips
450g (1lb) rice, cooked and cooled
Salt to taste
5ml (1 tsp) freshly ground black
   pepper
45ml (3 tblsp) tomato ketchup
50g (2oz) frozen peas

Heat 15ml (1 tblsp) oil in the wok
and pour in the beaten eggs. Cook
to make a thin omelette. Cut into
thin strips. Heat 15ml (1 tblsp) oil
in the wok and stir fry the onion
for 2 minutes. Add the shrimps,
prawns and fish and stir fry for 3-4
minutes. Remove the fish mixture
to a plate. Heat the remaining oil in
the wok. Add half the spring
onions and the green pepper and
stir fry for 2 minutes. Add the rice
and season with salt and pepper.
Add the tomato ketchup, peas,
fried fish, prawns and shrimps. Add
the soya sauce and stir fry for 3
minutes. Serve with the egg strips
arranged on top of the rice.

Vegetable Rice

PREPARATION TIME: 10 minutes

COOKING TIME: 5-8 minutes

450g (1lb) rice, cooked
175g (6oz) Chinese cabbage or
   Chinese leaves, shredded
100g (4oz) sliced green beans
100g (4oz) frozen peas
3 spring onions, chopped
15ml (1 tblsp) light soya sauce
Salt to taste

Rinse the cooked rice in cold water
and drain. Put the moist rice into a
pan. Arrange the Chinese cabbage,
sliced beans, peas and onions on
top. Cover and cook over a gentle
heat for 4-6 minutes. Sprinkle with
soya sauce and add salt to taste.
Stir the vegetables evenly into the
rice and raise the heat for a few
seconds. Serve immediately.

Plain Fried Rice

PREPARATION TIME: 5 minutes,
plus cooling time

COOKING TIME: 10-11 minutes

450g (1lb) Patna or long grain rice
1.25ml (¼ tsp) monosodium
   glutamate
30ml (2 tblsp) oil
Salt

Wash the rice in 4-5 changes of
cold water. Drain the rice and put
into a large pan or wok. Add
sufficient cold water to come
2.5cm (1 inch) above the level of
the rice. Bring to the boil. Stir once
and reduce the heat to simmer.
Cover and cook gently for 5-7
minutes until the water has been

**This page: Vegetable Rice (top),
Assorted Meat Congee (centre
right) and Rice Supreme
(bottom).**

**Facing page: Yang Chow Fried
Rice (top), Plain Fried Rice
(centre left) and Rice with
Minced Beef (bottom).**

totally absorbed and the rice is separate and fluffy, with the necessary amount of stickiness to be handled by chopsticks. (If necessary cook for a little longer.) Spread the rice out on a tray and cool. Sprinkle with the monosodium glutamate. Heat the oil in a wok or large frying pan and add the rice. Stir fry for 1-2 minutes. Add salt to taste and stir fry for a further 1-2 minutes.

Yang Chow Fried Rice

PREPARATION TIME: 10 minutes
COOKING TIME: 6-8 minutes

45ml (3 tblsp) cooking oil
1 egg, beaten
100g (4oz) cooked meat, chopped (pork, lamb, beef)
100g (4oz) cooked prawns or shrimps, shelled and chopped
50g (2oz) shelled green peas
2 spring onions, chopped
450g (1lb) dry, cooked rice
Salt to taste
5ml (1 tsp) monosodium glutamate (optional)

Heat 15ml (1 tblsp) oil in a wok. Fry the beaten egg until set, and break into small lumps. Remove the egg. Add the remaining oil and fry the meat, shrimps, peas and onions for 1-2 minutes. Add the cooked rice and sprinkle with salt and monosodium glutamate. Fry for 3 minutes. Mix in the cooked egg and serve immediately.

Sizzling Rice or Singing Rice

PREPARATION TIME: 50 minutes
COOKING TIME: 2 hours, plus time for deep frying sizzling rice

100g (4oz) short grained rice

When rice is cooked, the crust that forms on the bottom of the pot can be dried and then deep fried. When it is immersed in gravy or soup it makes a sizzling noise, hence the name. Once made or collected, the rice crusts can be kept for months.

To Make a Rice Crust
Wash rice in 4-5 changes of water until the water runs clear. Drain the rice and put it into a pan with 300ml (½ pint) of water; bring to the boil. Reduce heat to low and cook for 20 minutes, simmering gently. Turn off the heat and let the rice stand covered for 25-30 minutes. Take a non-stick frying pan and transfer the rice to it. Spread evenly to a thickness of 1cm (½ inch). Cook on a very gentle heat for 40-50 minutes. Turn over and cook gently for another hour. The rice should be very dry. Break into 5cm (2 inch) squares and store in a glass jar with a lid.

To Cook Sizzling Rice
Pour oil into a pan to a depth of 5cm (2 inches) and bring to a moderately high temperature (190°C or 375°F). Add the rice squares and fry until golden brown. Remove and drain on kitchen paper. Serve with soup or any stir fried dish.

Shrimp Egg Rice

PREPARATION TIME: 20 minutes
COOKING TIME: 17-18 minutes

450g (1lb) long or medium grained rice
2 eggs
2.5ml (½ tsp) salt
60ml (4 tblsp) oil
2 spring onions, chopped
1 large onion, peeled and chopped
2 cloves garlic, peeled and chopped
100g (4oz) peeled shrimps
50g (2oz) shelled peas
30ml (2 tblsp) dark soya sauce

To Cook the Rice
Wash rice in 4-5 changes of water. Add cold water to 2.5cm (1 inch) above the rice level and bring to the boil. Stir once and reduce the heat to simmer. Cover the pan and gently cook the rice for 5-7 minutes until the rice is dry and the liquid has been totally absorbed. Remove from the heat, add cold water to cover and drain thoroughly. Spread the rice on a serving tray and separate the grains with a fork.

Beat the eggs in a bowl and season with a pinch of salt. Heat the wok and add 15ml (1 tblsp) oil. Add the onions and stir fry for 2 minutes. Add the beaten eggs. Allow to set slightly and then stir the mixture until it scrambles. Remove onto a plate. Heat the wok and add 15ml (1 tblsp) oil. Fry the garlic for 1 minute then add the shrimps and cook for 2 minutes. Add the peas, and stir fry for 1 minute. Remove

onto a plate. Heat the wok and add the remaining oil, a little salt to taste and the cooked rice. Stir fry to heat the rice through. Stir in the soya sauce, shrimp mixture and the cooked eggs, gently stirring the mixture to blend. Serve immediately.

Shrimp Egg Rice (below), Sizzling Rice or Singing Rice (bottom left) and Plain Rice (bottom right).

Plain Rice

PREPARATION TIME: 5 minutes	
COOKING TIME: 5-7 minutes	

450g (1lb) rice
Pinch salt
10ml (2 tsp) oil

To make a bowl of plain rice, take any grade of long or medium grained rice. Wash the rice in 4-5 changes of water and then add enough cold water to come 2.5cm (1 inch) above the rice level. Add the salt and oil and bring to the boil. Stir once. Cover and simmer gently for 5-7 minutes until the water has been totally absorbed. Remove from the heat and serve. Plain boiled rice should be fluffy, yet have enough moisture around the rice so that the grains can be picked up easily by chopsticks.

Noodles in Soup

PREPARATION TIME: 10 minutes	
COOKING TIME: 6-8 minutes	

450g (1lb) small rounds of noodle cakes.
Salt
1.3 litres (2¼ pints) chicken or beef broth, or thick stock
100g (4oz) cooked shredded chicken
2 eggs, hard boiled and sliced
100g (4oz) Chinese napa cabbage, finely shredded (or iceberg lettuce)
2 spring onions, thinly sliced

2 sticks celery, chopped
50g (2oz) leek, chopped
2 spring onions, shredded
60ml (4 tblsp) stock
30ml (2 tblsp) soya sauce

Soak the rice noodles in warm water for 10-15 minutes. Drain thoroughly. Heat half the oil in a wok. Add the chicken, shrimps, bamboo shoots, celery, leeks and spring onions and stir fry for 2-3 minutes. Add the stock and salt and pepper to taste. Simmer for 2 minutes and then drain the chicken and vegetables. Heat the remaining oil, add the rice noodles and stir over the heat for 1 minute. Add the soya sauce and stir into the chicken and vegetable mixture. Cook together for 2-3 minutes. Serve immediately. Boiled prawns may also be added along with the chicken.

Meat and Prawn Chow Mein

PREPARATION TIME: 20 minutes

COOKING TIME: 12-15 minutes

450g (1lb) dried Chinese noodles or broken spaghetti
Salt to taste
60ml (4 tblsp) oil
2-3 spring onions, chopped
100g (4oz) cooked ham, shredded
100g (4oz) peeled prawns
100g (4oz) shredded carrots
100g (4oz) green beans, sliced
5ml (1 tsp) sugar
15ml (1 tblsp) rice wine or dry sherry
100g (4oz) cooked chicken, shredded
100g (4oz) bean sprouts
37ml (2½ tblsp) soya sauce

Cook the noodles in boiling, salted water for 4-5 minutes. Rinse under cold water and drain thoroughly. Toss in 15ml (1tblsp) oil. Heat the remaining oil in a wok. Add the onions, ham, prawns, carrots and green beans and stir fry for 2-3 minutes. Add the salt, sugar, wine, chicken and bean sprouts. Cook for 2 minutes. Add the cooked noodles and soya sauce. Cook for 1-2 minutes. Serve immediately.

Cook the noodles in boiling, salted water for 5 minutes. Drain thoroughly. Heat the broth or stock and add salt to taste. Serve the cooked noodles in bowls, and pour over the hot broth. Garnish with chicken, sliced eggs, cabbage and spring onions.

Stir Fried Shanghai Noodles

PREPARATION TIME: 10 minutes

COOKING TIME: 5-6 minutes

100g (4oz) white cabbage, shredded
2.5ml (½ tsp) sesame oil

45ml (3 tblsp) cooked oil
100g (4oz) cooked chicken or pork, shredded
450g (1lb) thick Shanghai noodles, cooked until just tender
30ml (2 tblsp) soya sauce
2.5ml (½ tsp) monosodium glutamate (optional)
Freshly ground black pepper to taste

Cook the cabbage in boiling water for 1 minute. Drain thoroughly. Heat the oils in a wok. Add the meat and stir fry for 2-3 minutes. Add the cooked noodles, soya sauce, monosodium glutamate and salt and pepper to taste. Add the cabbage, heat through and serve immediately.

Deep Fried Noodles
Boil noodles for 5 minutes. Drain thoroughly on absorbent paper. Deep fry in hot oil until crisp and golden.

Fried Rice Noodles

PREPARATION TIME: 25 minutes

COOKING TIME: 10 minutes

450g (1lb) rice noodles
45ml (3 tblsp) oil
100g (4oz) cooked chicken, shredded
50g (2oz) peeled shrimps
50g (2oz) bamboo shoots, sliced

This page: Deep Fried Noodles (top), Stir Fried Shanghai Noodles (centre), Fried Rice Noodles (bottom). Facing page: Meat and Prawn Chow Mein (top), Noodles in Soup (centre), Rice Noodles Singapore Style (bottom).

Rice Noodles Singapore Style

PREPARATION TIME: 15 minutes, plus soaking time for noodles

COOKING TIME: about 15 minutes

225g (8oz) rice noodles
Oil
2 eggs, beaten
1.25cm (½ inch) fresh root ginger, peeled and shredded
100g (4oz) bean sprouts
100g (4oz) cooked ham, pork or chicken, shredded
50g (2oz) chives, finely chopped
2 cloves garlic, finely chopped
Salt to taste
15ml (1 tblsp) chicken stock
30ml (2 tblsp) soya sauce
3 spring onions, chopped

Soak the rice noodles in warm water for 10 minutes and then drain well. Heat 15ml (1 tblsp) oil in a frying pan or wok and fry the beaten eggs to make a thin pancake. Slide onto a plate and cut into thin strips. Heat the wok or frying pan and add 15ml (1 tblsp) oil. Fry the ginger and bean sprouts for 2 minutes. Slide onto a plate. Heat the wok or frying pan with a further 15ml (1 tblsp) oil and fry the pork or chicken and the chives for 1-2 minutes. Slide onto a plate. Heat 30ml (2 tblsp) oil in the wok or frying pan and brown the garlic. Add the rice noodles and stir fry for 2-3 minutes. Add salt to taste, chicken stock, bean sprouts and pork or chicken. Mix well, sprinkle with soya sauce and stir over the heat for 1 minute. Top with the strips of egg pancake and spring onions and serve immediately.

Noodles with Beef and Almonds

PREPARATION TIME: 15 minutes

COOKING TIME: 10 minutes

45ml (3 tblsp) oil
1 onion, chopped
4 cloves of garlic, chopped
2.5cm (1 inch) fresh root ginger, peeled and sliced
225g (8oz) beef, thinly sliced
50g (2oz) carrots, diced
50g (2oz) sliced green beans
50g (2oz) water chestnuts, sliced
50g (2oz) mushrooms, sliced
2 green chillis, sliced in half
Salt

5ml (1 tsp) sugar
5ml (1 tsp) monosodium glutamate (optional)
250ml (8 fl oz) chicken stock
100g (4oz) blanched almonds
450g (1lb) noodles, cooked until just tender

Heat 30ml (2 tblsp) oil in a wok. Fry the onion, garlic, ginger and beef for 3 minutes. Add the carrots and green beans and fry for 2 minutes. Add the water chestnuts, mushrooms and green chillis and fry for 1 minute. Add salt, sugar, MSG and stock. Simmer for 1 minute. Remove to a dish and keep warm. Clean the wok and add the remaining oil. Fry the almonds and noodles for 1-2 minutes. Mix with the cooked vegetables and season with soya sauce. Serve immediately.

Egg Noodles with Meat Sauce

PREPARATION TIME: 15 minutes

COOKING TIME: 20-22 minutes

45ml (3 tblsp) oil
3 cloves garlic, chopped
2.5cm (1 inch) fresh root ginger, peeled and shredded
1 onion, chopped
1 green pepper, seeded and sliced
450g (1lb) beef mince
2.5ml (½ tsp) salt
10ml (2 tsp) tomato purée
15ml (1 tblsp) soya sauce
2.5ml (½ tsp) freshly ground black pepper
120ml (4 fl oz) chicken stock
5ml (1 tsp) cornflour
450g (1lb) egg noodles
2 spring onions, chopped

Heat 30ml (2 tblsp) oil in a wok. Fry the garlic and ginger for 1-2 minutes. Add the onion and fry for 2-3 minutes. Add the green pepper and the beef mince and fry for 1 minute. Add half the salt, tomato purée, soya sauce and ground pepper. Fry for a further 3 minutes. Blend the stock and cornflour and add to the wok. Cook until thickened and the meat is tender. Meanwhile, cook noodles in boiling, salted water for 3-4 minutes, and drain. Rinse in cold

water and drain once again. Heat the remaining oil in a pan. Add the noodles and toss over the heat until heated through. Arrange on a plate and top with the meat sauce. Garnish with chopped spring onions.

Fried Noodles with Shredded Chicken

PREPARATION TIME: 15 minutes

COOKING TIME: about 10 minutes

Oil
225g (8oz) cooked chicken, shredded
1 clove of garlic, chopped
2-3 spring onions, chopped
100g (4oz) whole green beans (or long Chinese beans, cut into 7.5cm (3 inch) pieces)
450g (1lb) noodles, cooked until just tender
15ml (1 tblsp) cornflour
250ml (8 fl oz) chicken stock
15ml (1 tblsp) soya sauce
15ml (1 tblsp) oyster sauce
5ml (1 tsp) wine
5ml (1 tsp) sugar
1.25ml (¼ tsp) salt

Heat 30ml (2 tblsp) oil in a wok and cook the chicken for 2 minutes. Remove the chicken. Add the garlic, spring onions and beans and fry for 2 minutes. Remove the vegetables. Heat 30ml (2 tblsp) oil in the wok and toss the pre-boiled noodles over the heat for 2 minutes. Arrange on a plate and keep warm. Return the fried chicken, onion and green beans to the wok and stir fry for 1 minute. Dissolve the cornflour in the chicken stock and add to the wok. Add the soya sauce, oyster sauce, wine, sugar and salt and pepper to taste. Simmer until the sauce is thick. Pour over the bed of noodles and serve immediately.

This page: Noodles with Beef and Almonds (top), Egg Noodles with Meat Sauce (centre) and Fried Noodles with Shredded Chicken (bottom).

Facing page: Chinese Bean Buns (top), Red Bean Filled Dim Sums (centre right) and Candied Apples (bottom).

Sweets

a chopstick on each circle of dough to mark it in half, and then in half again. Cut along the marks to within ⅓ of the centre. Place one portion of filling in the centre of the dough circle and fold the cut ends in to meet in the centre, to form a rosette. Secure by pinching ends of dough together. Place a piece of greased foil over the pinched ends and place the buns on a greased baking tray. Brush with a little milk. Bake at 190°C, 375°F, Gas Mark 5 for 20-25 minutes.

Red Bean Filled Dim Sums

PREPARATION TIME: 45-50 minutes

COOKING TIME: 10-12 minutes

50g (2oz) sugar
300ml (½ pint) warm water
15ml (1 tblsp) dried yeast
450g (1lb) plain flour
30ml (2 tblsp) melted lard
1 egg white, beaten

Filling
275g (10oz) sweet bean paste, ready made
Red food colouring

Dissolve the sugar in the warm water and add the yeast. Stir until dissolved. Leave in a warm place until frothy. Sift the flour into a mixing bowl and add the melted lard and the yeast mixture. Mix together. Turn the mixture onto a floured surface and knead to a smooth and elastic dough. Roll into a long sausage and divide into 24 equal portions. Roll each portion into a 5cm (2 inch) flat circle. Brush edges of dough with beaten egg white. Place 15ml (1 tblsp) of filling into the centre of each circle and pull the dough around it to enclose the filling. Pleat the open edges in a circular fashion, so that a small opening is left in the middle of the pleating. Place a small piece of greased foil over the pleats on each dim sum. Leave for 10-12 minutes until the dough becomes springy to the touch. Put a dab of red food

Chinese Bean Buns

PREPARATION TIME: about 2 hours, including proving time

COOKING TIME: about 30 minutes

60ml (2 fl oz) milk
50g (2 oz) sugar
2.5ml (½ tsp) salt
25g (1oz) lard
60ml (2 fl oz) warm water
10ml (2 tsp) dried yeast
1 egg, beaten
275g (10oz) plain flour

Bring the milk almost to the boil. Stir in the sugar, salt and lard. Cool slightly. Put the warm water and yeast into a bowl and stir to mix. Add the lukewarm milk mixture. Add the beaten egg and 225g (8oz) of the flour and beat until smooth. Add the remaining flour and mix to a dough. Turn dough out onto a well-floured board and knead until smooth and elastic. Place in a greased bowl. Brush the dough with oil and cover. Leave to rise in a warm place until doubled in size (about 1 hour).

Filling
100g (4oz) sweet bean paste
25g (1oz) sugar
25g (1oz) chopped walnuts
15ml (1 tblsp) lard

Heat the filling ingredients together in a wok for 5-6 minutes until smooth and shiny. Remove and cool. Divide the filling into 12-14 portions. Knead the risen dough again for 2 minutes and then divide the dough into 12-14 portions. Flatten into thick, circular shapes 10cm (4 inches) in diameter. Place

colouring on each dim sum. Arrange the dim sums in a bamboo steaming basket and steam over boiling water for 10-12 minutes. The dim sums are ready when they are dry and smooth. Alternatively they can be baked at 180°C, 350°F, Gas Mark 4, for about 20 minutes.

Agar-Agar Pudding

PREPARATION TIME: 5 minutes

COOKING TIME: 4-5 minutes

600ml (1 pint) milk
100g (4oz) sugar
25g (1oz) ground almonds
50g (2oz) agar-agar (also called Chinese grass)
25g (1oz) blanched and chopped almonds

Mix the milk, sugar and ground almonds together in a pan and stir over the heat for 4 minutes. Add the agar-agar and stir until dissolved. Stir in the chopped almonds. Pour into a shallow dish 2.5cm (1 inch) deep. Cool and keep in refrigerator until set. Serve chilled, cut into diamond or square shapes.

Almond Cookies
Makes 60 cookies

PREPARATION TIME: 20 minutes

COOKING TIME: 12-15 minutes

225g (8oz) lard
100g (4oz) caster sugar
50g (2oz) brown sugar
1 egg, beaten
Few drops almond essence
275g (10oz) plain flour
Pinch salt
7.5ml (1½ tsp) baking powder
75g (3oz) blanched almonds
1 egg yolk
30ml (2 tblsp) water

Cream the lard with the caster sugar and the brown sugar until light and fluffy. Add the egg and almond essence and beat until smooth. Sift the flour, salt and baking powder. Mix the dry ingredients into the creamed mixture. Shape into small balls on a lightly floured surface. Flatten slightly and press an almond into the centre of each one. Place onto a greased baking sheet. Mix the egg yolk with the water. Brush the cookies with the egg glaze. Bake at 180°C, 350°F, Gas Mark 4, for 12-15 minutes.

Sweet Almond Pudding

PREPARATION TIME: 4-5 minutes

COOKING TIME: 6 minutes

175g (6oz) blanched almonds
450ml (¾ pint) water
175g (6oz) sugar
45ml (3 tblsp) rice powder, or ground rice
150ml (¼ pint) milk

Blend the blanched almonds and water in the liquidiser. Put into a pan and bring to the boil. Add the sugar and stir over the heat until the sugar has dissolved. Add the rice slowly to the milk and stir gradually into the simmering sugar and almond mixture. Cook gently until the mixture thickens. Remove from the heat and pour into a serving dish. Serve hot or cold.

Sweet Dumplings

PREPARATION TIME: 10 minutes

COOKING TIME: 15-20 minutes

Oil
75g (3oz) sugar
100g (4oz) plain red bean paste
50g (2oz) desiccated coconut
4 egg whites
15ml (1 tblsp) plain flour
45ml (3 tblsp) cornflour
Icing sugar

Heat 15ml (1 tblsp) oil in a wok and add the sugar, bean paste and coconut. Stir fry for 4-5 minutes until the sugar melts and the paste is smooth and shiny. Fry for a few minutes more and then allow to cool on a dish. Whisk the egg whites until stiff and mix with the plain flour and cornflour to a smooth batter. Beat well. Clean the wok and heat sufficient oil for deep frying. Make 10-12 even-sized balls from the bean paste mixture. Dip each ball into the batter and then

deep fry for 3-4 minutes until golden and crisp. Fry a few at a time and drain on kitchen paper. Dust with icing sugar before serving.

Stuffed Lychees

PREPARATION TIME: 20 minutes

450g (1lb) canned lychees, stones removed
225g (8oz) canned pineapple rings
Few drops vanilla essence or almond essence

Drain the lychees into a bowl, reserving the juice. Drain the pineapple rings and reserve the liquid. Slice each pineapple ring into 2.5cm (½ inch) long strips. Press one or two strips of pineapple into each lychee. Arrange the pineapple-filled lychees in a deep serving dish. Mix the pineapple and lychee liquid with a few drops of essence. Spoon over the stuffed fruits. Serve well chilled. Alternatively, stuff the lychees with maraschino cherries, mango, canned pears, oranges etc.

Facing page: Sweet Dumplings (top), Almond Cookies (centre left) and Date Cake (bottom right).

Glossary

Agar-agar: this is a specially prepared, dried seaweed which is sold in the shops as Chinese grass. The white, fibrous strands require soaking and are used like gelatine. Agar-agar is also sold in ground, powder form. It is used for puddings and as a setting agent. All Chinese and Oriental shops sell it.

Anise, star: this is an eight pointed clove with a strong anise smell and flavour, and is one of the spices which goes into 'Chinese five spice' powder. It can be purchased in powder or whole form. It is used to flavour red-cooked poultry and many meat dishes.

Bean curd (Tau fu): this comes in soft, custard-like squares and is made from soya beans. It is highly nutritious and is one of the most important Chinese foods. It is available only from Chinese grocers and is also sold in dried form as bean curd stick, in brine, and fried.

Bean pastes: sauces made from soya beans which are sold in cans and jars. Once opened, they should be kept refrigerated. There are many varieties of bean paste:
Hot bean paste, which is made with chillis and is salty.
Soya bean paste, which is dark in colour, very salty and is made with fermented soya beans.
Sweet bean paste, which is made with black soya beans, sugar, flour and spices.
Yellow bean paste, which is made with yellow soya beans and this too is quite salty in taste.

Bean sprouts: these are shoots of mung beans or soya beans. The soya beans are stronger in flavour. They are readily available from most supermarkets and Oriental shops. Fresh bean sprouts will keep for several days if refrigerated in a perforated plastic bag; discard any discoloured shoots. The topped and tailed sprouts are known as 'Silver Sprouts' and are used for very special dishes.

Black bean sauce: this can be bought ready made from shops, or made with 45-60ml (3-4 tblsp) steamed, black soya beans mixed to a paste with 30ml (2 tblsp) oil and 30ml (2 tblsp) sugar.

Broccoli, Chinese: a dark green, leafy vegetable which bears small white flowers; it looks very much like miniature broccoli. It is sold only in Chinese grocers and, if not available, it can be substituted by Chinese cabbage or ordinary broccoli.

Cabbage, Chinese white: there are two main varieties. One is called Pak-choy, and the other, a more tender flowering white cabbage, is called Choy-sum. Chinese leaves and Tientsin cabbage are sold in supermarkets and Oriental shops and also in many fruit and vegetable markets. Chinese leaves are tightly packed and have creamy white leaves with a thick central stalk. They are often used in salads in place of lettuce. All these cabbages can be substituted by ordinary cabbage.

Chestnuts, water: these are the bulb-like stems of the bulrush. They are slightly sweet and have a crisp texture. They are usually sold in cans; occasionally they are sold in their natural form. They are available from some supermarkets and all Oriental and Chinese shops. Canned water chestnuts will keep for 3-4 weeks after opening, if refrigerated and kept in water. The water should be changed daily. Chestnuts are also ground to a flour, which is used for making batter.

Chilli oil: this can be bought ready-prepared. Chilli oil can also be made by infusing dried chillis in hot vegetable oil, but it will not keep for as long as the ready-prepared variety.

Chilli sauce: this is a very hot, spicy and tangy sauce made from chillis and vinegar. Chilli sauce can be easily purchased from many supermarkets and all Chinese grocers. It is used to season a wide variety of savoury Chinese dishes.

Chinese wine: there are many kinds of wine made from rice. Chinese rice wine can be substituted by ordinary dry sherry in most recipes. Rice wines vary considerably in quality, but they are all very strong.

Cloud ear: this is known by many names e.g. wood ear, snow fungus, sea jelly or jelly sheet. It is actually a dried fungus which, when soaked in water, resembles a puffed ear, hence the name. It has no flavour and is used only to add texture to a dish. It will keep for a month in its dried form.

Cooked oil: many Chinese dishes require cooked oil in the recipe. It is made by heating vegetable, peanut or any other kind of oil until it smokes.

Dates: these are sold in dried form and will keep for a month. There are two varieties, black and red, and they can be purchased from most Oriental shops. They resemble dried prunes. They are used in sweet, and some savoury, stir fried dishes. Ordinary dried dates can easily be used in their place.

Fennel (dried): this is sold in seed form and the tiny, pale green seeds resemble caraway seeds. Fennel is sold in supermarkets, health food shops and in Chinese grocery shops and is an important ingredient in five-spice powder.

Five-spice powder: this is a strong, coffee-coloured seasoning made with equal parts of fagara (brown peppercorns), cinnamon bark, clove, fennel and star anise. All the spices are ground to a fine powder and it is used sparingly.

Flour: many varieties of flour are used in Chinese cookery, the main one being the ordinary unleavened flour, which is usually a finely ground wheat flour. It is used to make most steamed breads and some pastries.

High gluten flour: this is used to make wonton wrappers. It is a strong flour with a high gluten content and can therefore be rolled very thinly.

Tang flour: this is made from a low-gluten wheat. The flour is used for making clear wrappers for 'dim sum'; when cooked, this flour becomes transparent.

Ginger: fresh root ginger is a vital ingredient in Chinese cooking; nearly all the traditional meat and fish dishes use root ginger. Sprouting ginger is the best and it is used for preserving foods in vinegar and for pickling. The tough, older roots are strong in flavour. The texture may be fibrous but if you chop the ginger finely with a sharp knife it will release its full flavour. Ginger not only gives a distinct flavour to a dish but it helps the digestion as well. Fresh ginger cannot be substituted by ground or preserved ginger. It is widely available.

Glutinous rice: this is also known as 'sticky' rice. It is a special variety of Chinese rice which has opaque grains, and when cooked turns transparent and very sticky. It is used for making both puddings and savoury dishes.

Hoi Sin sauce: this is a sweet, brownish-red sauce made from soya beans, salt, sugar, chilli, garlic, vinegar and flour. It has a sweet, tangy flavour and it can be bought from Chinese or large supermarkets. It is used in cooking as well as being served as a dip for meats etc. It is also known as seafood sauce or barbecue sauce.

Long beans: these are one of the many typical Chinese vegetables. As the name suggests, they are longer than the ordinary beans. They are obtainable from most Chinese shops and from Oriental grocers. They can be substituted by lobia beans or ordinary green beans (string beans).

Maltose: a molasses-like substance which is made by fermenting barley or a similar grain. It is also known as malt sugar, and can be substituted in recipes by honey, treacle or golden syrup.

Melon, winter: this is a very large, green-skinned melon with a soft, white flesh and a delicate taste. It is sold fresh in Chinese shops or Oriental grocers but can also be purchased cubed in cans. Peeled and seeded marrow or cucumber can be used as a substitute.

Monosodium glutamate: this is a white, crystalline substance commonly known as MSG. It is used extensively in Chinese cookery·for tenderising meat and for enhancing the flavour of dishes. It is sometimes sold under the names of Aji No Moto and Vi Tsin and is also called the 'taste powder'. It should be used sparingly, as too much will spoil the dish, and can be totally omitted from recipes if preferred.

Mooli: mooli or muli is a crisp, white variety of radish. It grows to about 25cm (10 inches) in length and 10cm (4 inches) in diameter. It is stronger than the ordinary red radish and is eaten in salads and as a vegetable. It has a sharp, crunchy texture and flavour.

Mushrooms: there are many varieties of dried mushrooms which are used in Chinese cooking. Follow the recipe to see the type suggested. To prepare dried mushrooms for cooking, soak in hot water for ½ hour. Drain and season with 7.5ml (½ tblsp) wine and a little sugar. (See also Chinese mushrooms and cloud ear.)

Mustard green: this is also known as leaf mustard. It has a slightly bitter taste and is crunchy in texture. It is used in soups and stir fried dishes. It is only sold in Oriental and Chinese grocery shops. Use broccoli as the nearest substitute.

Noodles: there are many different kinds of noodles. Some are made from wheat flour, some from rice flour and some from bean flour.

Bean thread noodles: thin, white, transparent noodles made from moong bean flour. They should be soaked before use. Cake noodles: these are bound together in tight balls.

Rice sheet noodles: these are made from rice and come in wide, flat sheets. They are also sold in dried form.

Rice stick noodles: (sometimes called rice vermicelli) these are very thin noodles made from rice, and they are soaked in hot water for 10-12 minutes before use. If deep fried they become very light and crisp, like wafers.

Shanghai noodles, thin: these are mostly used in soups and are thin and pale in colour. The basic noodles are made from wheat flour.

Shanghai noodles, thick: these are yellowish in colour and are made from wheat flour enriched with egg. Commonly sold in dried form, in the shape of small and large cakes, they are also sold fresh in Chinese shops; these fresh noodles can be kept in plastic bags in the refrigerator for up to 1 week. All these varieties of noodles are obtainable from Chinese and Oriental grocers, and many are sold in supermarkets and other food shops. Noodles can be substituted by spaghetti, though the flavour will not be the same.

Oyster sauce: this is a special sauce produced from soya sauce and oysters which have been fermented together. It is used as a flavouring and as a colouring and also as a condiment. Once opened it will keep in the bottle for several months.

Parsley (Chinese): otherwise known as fresh coriander, this is a herb of Indian origin, which is used as a flavouring and a garnish. The flat leaves have a strong flavour and can not be substituted by Western parsley.

Preserved Chinese vegetables: these are specially prepared dried vegetables, which retain their original flavour. Preserved vegetables are also sold in cans and jars, packed in a brine solution.

Rice: there are many different varieties of rice. Long grained rice

is the variety usually used for making simple rice dishes, but a special, glutinous, medium-grain rice is used for making puddings and savoury dishes.

Sesame oil: an aromatic oil produced from sesame seeds. This has a special flavour and is used both as a seasoning and as a vital ingredient in some sauces. Sold in bottles, it is available from most general grocery, chemist and health food shops.

Sesame seeds: there are two varieties of these tiny seeds. One is white and the other black. Both are used for garnishes, as well as for making pastes, sweets and fillings and can be purchased from Oriental and Chinese grocers.

Snow peas (mange tout): these are delicate, flat pea pods and the whole vegetable is eaten. They are either eaten raw or lightly cooked and they add character and colour to many dishes. Will keep for a few days if kept in perforated plastic bags in the refrigerator.

Soya sauce: there are two kinds of soya sauce; one is dark and the other is light. Both are used for flavouring soups, stir fried dishes and for seasoning nearly all Chinese foods. They are extracts made from fermented soya beans. The dark soya sauce is stronger in flavour and thicker and the lighter varieties are the weaker infusions of the fermented beans. The first extract is the strongest and the best. Soya sauces are sometimes flavoured with mushrooms, oysters and shrimp roe, to give them added flavour.

Spring onions: these are sometimes called scallions and are used extensively in Chinese cooking. They are different from the purple variety of long onion.

Stocks: Chinese cooking needs stock of one sort or another in almost all dishes. There are two main kinds of stock that are used. It is very useful to make home-made stock and keep it refrigerated for 5-7 days.

Superior stock or strong stock: 1 boiling chicken, 100g (4oz) loin of pork, cubed, 25g (1oz) Yunnan ham, cubed, 2 litres (3½ pints) water, 1 cm (½ inch) fresh root ginger, peeled and thinly sliced, 2 spring onions, chopped, salt, freshly ground black pepper. Place chicken, pork and ham into a pan with the water and bring to the boil. Cook for 10 minutes and skim. Add ginger, spring onions and season with salt and pepper. Simmer for 1½ hours. The fat should not be skimmed off completely as this gives the stock its characteristic flavour.

Tangerine peel, dried: the best sun-dried peels are several years old. Peel is used as a seasoning for stews and other dishes. It is a little expensive, however, and can be omitted from the recipe, or substituted by home dried peels.

Vinegar: Chinese vinegars are made from fermented rice, by the process of distillation, and there are four main varieties:

Black vinegar: this is similar to malt vinegar, but not quite so strong. It has a stronger flavour than other Chinese varieties, and is used as a flavouring and as a condiment.

Red vinegar: this is distinctly red in colour as the name suggests, and is used particularly with seafood dishes and as a condiment.

Sweet vinegar: this is almost like port in flavour, very sweet and rich black in colour. It is used mainly for braised and stewed dishes and has a sharp taste.

White vinegar: this is not as strong as European white vinegar; it is more tangy, yet milder. When substituting one vinegar for another taste carefully.

Yunnan ham: this is a special kind of Chinese smoked ham which is produced by a salting and smoking process. Substitute: good cuts of European smoked ham, smoked gammon or lean rashers of smoked bacon.

Index